• DISCOVERING THE

THE BOSTON
HARBOR ISLANDS

CHRISTOPHER KLEIN

THIRD EDITION

Globe
Pequot

Guilford, Connecticut

Globe
Pequot

An imprint of The Rowman & Littlefield Publishing Group, Inc.
4501 Forbes Blvd., Ste. 200
Lanham, MD 20706
www.rowman.com

Distributed by NATIONAL BOOK NETWORK

British Library Cataloguing in Publication Information available

Library of Congress Cataloging-in-Publication Data available

ISBN 978-1-4930-5039-0 (paperback)
ISBN 978-1-4930-5040-6 (e-book)

♾️™ The paper used in this publication meets the minimum requirements of American National Standard for Information Sciences—Permanence of Paper for Printed Library Materials, ANSI/NISO Z39.48-1992.

sebatl/Getty Images

Contents

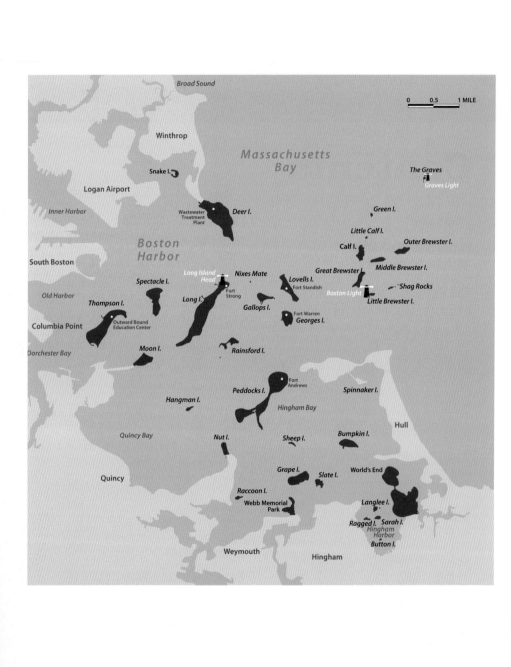

Icon Key

ACCESS

 FERRY / INTER-ISLAND FERRY

 PRIVATE CRAFT ONLY

 ACCESS DISCOURAGED/ RESTRICTED

 CAR / PARKING

 MARINA / MOORINGS

 DOG FRIENDLY

SIGHTS

 LIGHTHOUSE

 FORT

 HISTORIC STRUCTURES & RUINS

 ARTS & CULTURE

 SPECIAL INTEREST

ACTIVITIES

 CAMPING

 HIKING / WALKING TRAILS

 LIFE-GUARDED BEACH

 FISHING

 BIRDING

 KAYAKING

SERVICES

 FOOD

 TOILETS

 INFORMATION / RANGER STAFFED

Portrait of the Harbor: An Introduction

AS THE CROWD BOARDS THE FERRY AT BOSTON'S LONG WHARF, a sense of anticipation mingles with the smells of salt water and suntan lotion filling the air. Young children tote their sand pails. Their parents carry coolers with picnic supplies. Intrepid campers haul their gear and tents. The women of the Red Hat Society scour the itinerary for their afternoon outing. It's a diverse crowd, to be sure, but they all have one thing in common: they're embarking on an island adventure.

Within moments, the ferry is underway, passing the burgeoning Seaport District and gliding underneath the bellies of jumbo jets landing at Logan Airport. Seagoing vessels of all varieties crowd the harbor. The spire of the Old North Church, the tower of the Custom House, and the rest of the city skyline dissolve in the mist, and a cool sea breeze tempers the sultry summer heat.

In no time at all the passengers arrive at their destination: Spectacle Island. It's a completely different world from the one they just left. The canyon walls of Boston's skyscrapers have been replaced by open skies. The chaos of the city streets has been supplanted by the tranquility of island life.

What is it about islands that speaks to the adventurer in each of us? Why do we experience such a thrill at being surrounded by water, cut off

FERRY SERVICE

At the time of publication, there is ferry service to seven of the thirty-four harbor islands. Spectacle and Georges are considered hub islands. Ferry service leaves from Long Wharf in Boston to Georges and Spectacle Islands, and from the Hingham Shipyard to Georges Island.

Inter-island ferry routes run from Georges Island to Spectacle, Lovells, and Peddocks Islands and from the Hingham Shipyard to Bumpkin, Grape, Peddocks, Georges, and Lovells Islands. Please ask the crew on board the mainland ferry about connecting to another island, as routes may change.

Timetables, fares, and information on free ferry days are available online at bostonharborislands.org, or call (617) 223-8666. The season runs from May to mid-October. (For Spectacle Island service from Winthrop and Squantum Point Park in Quincy, visit town.winthrop.ma.us/ferry.)

Special ferry service is provided to Thompson Island. See that chapter for additional information.

A boat on Boston Harbor sails by Nixes Mate.

from the rest of the world? Isolated and remote, romantic and invigorating, islands offer the promise of solitude and exploration as well as an intimate communion with the natural world in one of its most extreme designs. Few landscapes possess the same drama, magic, or mystery, and as the waves crest along the shoreline, life and its innumerable routines are somehow put into perspective. Perhaps the mystery lies in the voyage itself. Whether you opt for the ferry, a kayak, or your own ship, the effort required to land on an island is integral to the overall experience. These miniature worlds, formed by a complex of geological forces, call on us to interact with our environment in ways that are increasingly less frequent.

Spectacle Island is just one of the jewels in the Boston Harbor Islands national park area, which includes thirty-four islands and coastal peninsulas in a twelve-mile radius from downtown Boston. And it is just one of thirty-four chances from which to see Boston in a new light. Long before Frederick Law Olmsted conceived of his Emerald Necklace of parkland ringing Boston, the Boston Harbor Islands formed a "Sapphire Necklace" draped around Boston Neck—the narrow peninsula on which Boston was originally built. No other major city in the United States is blessed with such an island-studded harbor.

MARINAS AND ISLAND MOORINGS

Moorings are available at Spectacle, Gallops, Georges, and Peddocks Islands. Reservations for day and overnight use can be made through Dockwa at dockwa.com or through the Dockwa app. With the exception of Spectacle Island, docks are for passenger pick-up and drop-off only. For more information, visit bostonharborislands.org/boating.

More than one hundred thousand people a year travel by ferry to the harbor islands, drawn by the rare opportunity to visit unspoiled landscapes and wildlife features within the confines of an urban center. This urban oasis is an area of breathtaking beauty and spectacular vistas. Filled with colorful tales of hermits, ghosts, pirates, shipwrecks, and buried treasure, the ruins of forts and summer estates fascinate explorers of all ages. Like the ebbing and flowing tide, the city's history laps up on their shores, and the harbor islands are a prism through which we can view the history of Boston and, to a large extent, the United States.

It's not too grand a statement to say that Boston would not be the city it is today without its harbor islands. In fact, the islands built John Winthrop's nascent "city upon a hill." Colonists harvested timber from the mature forests that grew on the islands to construct homes and wharves. The slate quarried from their shores paved the city streets. Livestock that grazed and crops that grew on the denuded harbor islands fed the growing colony. What's more, the islands afforded Boston protection from nature's fury and enemy attack, creating one of the safest and most commodious harbors in the world, which in turn allowed Boston to become a thriving maritime power.

Indeed, nature proved to be a fine engineer when she designed Boston Harbor and sculpted its island cluster. The massive glaciers that engulfed Boston during the Ice Age more than fifteen thousand years ago left behind smooth mounds of sand, gravel, and rock called "drumlins"—in profile, they've been described as upside-down teaspoons. As the ice sheets melted, the water level rose, and the drumlins were surrounded by Boston Harbor, formed between the two outstretched arms of Winthrop and Hull that seem to clutch the islands in their warm embrace. (Bunker Hill and Beacon Hill are both drumlins as well.) Afloat within the vast estuary ecosystem formed by the salty Massachusetts Bay and the freshwater of the Charles, Mystic, and Neponset Rivers, the Boston Harbor Islands are a geological rarity, forming the only drumlin "swarm" in the United States that intersects a coastline.

While the harbor islands have created natural breakwaters that bear the brunt of ferocious gales and the open sea, they have also provided easily defensible locations to protect Boston from enemy attack. From the establishment of a fort on Castle Island in 1634 until just after World War II, the Boston Harbor Islands were home to active military fortifications that deterred potential naval incursions, trained soldiers, and housed prisoners of war. In their darkest moment, the islands were used during King Philip's War in 1675 and 1676 to intern Native Americans.

For centuries, the Boston Harbor Islands have served as a gateway to Boston and America. For more than three hundred years, the towering beacon of Boston Light on Little Brewster Island, the oldest light station in America, has been a welcome sight for thousands of tempest-tossed mariners arriving from around the world. Today, of course, most visitors to Boston arrive by air, but the islands outside the cabin windows still greet this new generation of travelers who touch down along the harbor shores at Logan Airport.

A sailboat heads to the Outer Harbor.

Beginning in the 1840s, for the tens of thousands of immigrants starting a new life in a new land, the first piece of American soil on which these "huddled masses" stepped was often at the quarantine and immigration stations on the islands. In fact, so many immigrants passed through the Boston Harbor Islands that they were considered as an alternative site for the Statue of Liberty when New York City was having trouble raising money to build its pedestal in the early 1880s.

The rise in immigration nearly doubled the population of Boston between 1840 and 1860, and those seeking relief from the congested city sought out recreational activities in the harbor and on its islands. Island inns and resorts popped up during the nineteenth century. Summer colonies took root. And steamships crisscrossed the harbor bringing day trippers to and from island destinations. While most Bostonians took to the harbor to enjoy its cool, salubrious breezes, others sought out activities that were frowned upon by puritanical Boston. These remote, offshore locations provided the perfect venues for unsanctioned boxing matches, gambling, and opium parties.

Boston also turned to its harbor islands as a place to exile its sick and downtrodden and house its social institutions. The islands provided faraway places to sequester people and material that Bostonians didn't want in the

Sailboats head to the outer harbor.

city proper. In this regard, the history of the islands is very much the history of Boston's reform impulse. Asylums, poorhouses, hospitals, and prisons were situated on many of the harbor islands. Likewise, as many as four islands were the home to quarantine stations, which protected the city from outbreaks of smallpox and other deadly, contagious diseases. Many victims of those diseases died on the islands, and today these forgotten cemeteries are as common as the ruins of old military installations.

Of course, as Bostonians know all too well, long before the colonists dumped their tea into the harbor, they were draining their sewage into it. The city also sent its garbage to the islands, and the Spectacle Island landfill is perhaps the most notorious example of the disregard Bostonians had for their islands and waterways. Centuries of this environmental degradation took their toll on the health of the harbor and its aquatic life, and by 1987, the water quality in Boston Harbor was so poor that the federal government identified it as the dirtiest in America. The banner headline across the top of the *Boston Herald* on April 28, 1987, said it all: "Harbor of Shame."

Though it's hard to fathom given the level of pollution, the islands were the last open frontier available for the continuing sprawl of Boston and under the threat of development throughout the 1960s and 1970s. The most sweeping proposal called for the construction of a high-rise apartment community—connected to downtown by subways, ferries, and bridges—that could house as many as 150,000 people. There were also proposals, building on Boston's long tradition of land-making, to fill in the harbor around some of the islands to build a new airport and a world's fair site. Islands—such as Apple, Bird, and Governor's—were indeed lost to this practice, and now remain buried somewhere beneath Logan Airport.

Luckily, the Boston Harbor Islands had their champions who fought to prevent development, clean up the harbor, and preserve their exquisite natural beauty. One of the most significant was the late Edward Rowe Snow, the master storyteller and historian who wrote dozens of books on New England maritime history, many of which included stories about Boston Harbor and its islands. Through his writings and radio programs, Snow brought the lively history and legends surrounding the islands to the attention of a new generation of Bostonians. No one who followed Snow on his tour through the dark corridors of Fort Warren will forget his tale of the Lady in Black.

Taking up Snow's mantle, advocates of the harbor and the islands successfully pressed in federal court during the 1980s for the $4.5 billion cleanup of Boston Harbor, the centerpiece of which was the new waste-water treatment plant on Deer Island that opened in 2001. Ruling that "the law secures to the people the right to a clean harbor," federal district court judge A. David Mazzone served as a mighty force overseeing the cleanup project for nearly two decades. The project has transformed the harbor from one of the dirtiest to one of the cleanest, and it has led to a rebirth of the islands. Likewise, another major Boston construction project, the Big Dig, transformed Spectacle Island from a garbage dump to the national park area's reborn jewel.

The cleanup of the harbor played a pivotal role in the creation of the Boston Harbor Islands National Recreation Area in 1996. (Native Americans objected to the term "recreation area" to describe the islands where their ancestors were incarcerated and died during King Philip's War, so the islands are now referred to as a "national park area.") The national park area is unique in that the National Park Service owns none of its 1,600 acres, and the islands are owned and maintained by a complex partnership of federal, state, city, and nonprofit agencies, which seeks to maintain the right balance between the islands' role as a source for recreation and a preserve for scenery, wildlife, and historic sites.

At the Boston Harbor Islands Welcome Center on the Rose Kennedy Greenway, visitors can get information about the national park area from park rangers and volunteers and view interpretive panels and a granite topographical map of the islands inlaid in the ground.

With the completion of the Big Dig and the blossoming of the Rose Kennedy Greenway, Boston is rediscovering its waterfront and its nautical heritage. At the Boston Harbor Islands Welcome Center on the Greenway, park rangers and interpretive panels enlighten a new generation to the endless number of adventures that can be found just a short boat ride away. History buffs can explore lighthouses, ruins, and the military installations that have protected Boston from the time of its founding through World War II. Adventure seekers can scuba dive amid centuries-old shipwrecks. Boaters can venture to the outer islands, a breathtaking ocean wilderness that marks the edge of civilization. Anglers can fish for striped bass, bluefish, and flounder in the revitalized harbor waters. The wandering trails on many of the islands are perfect for day-hikes, and several islands are available for overnight camping. Summer weekends provide a wide variety of cultural and educational programs—from old-time baseball games, jazz concerts, and art installations, to children's programs, citizen science activities, and ranger-led tours.

Nature lovers will be enthralled by the islands' diverse flora and fauna that thrive in a range of habitats from tidal salt marshes to rocky shores to woodlands. In many regards, the Boston Harbor Islands are New England's backyard Galapagos. With the loss of biodiversity on the planet at an all-time high, the harbor islands provide a natural laboratory for scientists and the public to explore nature's evolution and how multiple, diverse human impacts affect natural systems.

Visitors can get information about visiting the Boston Harbor Islands at the Welcome Center on the Rose Kennedy Greenway.

Botanists have identified more than five hundred plant species on the islands, many of them non-native due to changes in habitat caused by human deforestation or the introduction of invasive species. With more than two hundred species of birds, the Boston Harbor Islands are considered an Important Bird Area by organizations such as Mass Audubon. Small mammals, such as rabbits, raccoons, and foxes, have been found on the islands, and thanks to the cleanup of the harbor, seals and porpoises have returned to the outer islands. Humpback whales have been spotted splashing around in Boston Harbor, and tide pools along the shores are teeming with a micro-wilderness of aquatic life. These habitats serve as unique living classrooms for Boston-area schoolchildren brought to the islands by nonprofit groups and summer camps.

In some respects, the undeveloped landscapes on many islands make it easy to imagine what this part of the world looked like when the first group

GETTING THERE AND GOING ASHORE

A number of islands are open to visitation, but lack docks; boaters who would like to go ashore will often need a flat-bottom raft, dinghy, or kayak.

The beacons of Boston Light and Graves Light guard the two entrances to Boston Harbor.

Boston Harbor Islands
TOP TEN

1. Scale to the top of Boston Light. Take a guided tour of the oldest light station in the country and climb the seventy-six spiral steps and two short ladders to come face-to-face with the lighthouse's giant Fresnel lens.

2. Take a dip. Grab your bathing suit, towel, and suntan lotion and head to the sand and surf at Spectacle Island's life-guarded beach.

3. Wander Fort Warren's dark passages. Explore the spooky tunnels of this historic fort that once held Confederate prisoners during the Civil War.

4. Pitch a tent. Camp out on the islands and catch unforgettable sunrises and sunsets in the shadows of the city skyline. Spend the night on Grape Island for the most bucolic setting, or if "glamping" is more your style, rent one of the yurts with bunk beds and electricity on Peddocks Island.

5. Grab a paddle. Beginning kayakers can spend the afternoon exploring the Hingham Harbor islands, while experienced kayakers can brave the outer harbor to visit the Brewsters.

6. Scale Thompson Island's ropes and climbing walls. Participate in one of Outward Bound's programs and challenge your limitations by conquering the ropes course and climbing towers.

7. Pack a lunch. There are fantastic spots to picnic on all the harbor islands, but the picnic areas on Bumpkin and Great Brewster Islands offer unparalleled vistas.

8. Brush up on your fish tales. Fish populations are rebounding along with the harbor's water quality. Striped bass, bluefish, flounder, and cod are among the fish that are biting.

9. Follow your feathered friends. Grab a pair of binoculars and try to spot some of the two hundred species of birds that frequent the Boston Harbor Islands.

10. See Boston in a new light. There's no better view of the city and harbor than from Spectacle Island's 157-foot-high north drumlin.

of Puritans aboard the *Arbella* passed by in 1630. Since then, these islands have had a front-row seat for some of the most seminal moments in the long sweep of American history: A tea party in 1773, which rippled through the harbor and grew into waves of freedom washing over America. The departure of the last British troops driven out by a band of colonists in 1776. The arrival of the first "coffin ships" carrying Irish famine victims in Black '47. The launch of Donald McKay's fleet clippers, such as the *Flying Cloud*, that would rule the seas in the 1850s. And the return of the celebrated

54th Massachusetts Volunteer Infantry Regiment from bloody Civil War battlefields.

But there is a quieter history of the islands, too, though no less important, and it speaks to the bond between Bostonians and the sea. As the last frontier in the Boston area, the islands tell us about the peopling of New England. From the Native Americans who seasonally camped on the islands to the Portuguese fishermen who lived in shanties on their shores; from the Brahmins who built unapproachable estates high above the crashing waves to the hermits who lived like castaways—the harbor islands are awash in the history of hearty New Englanders drawn to the ocean.

Each island of Boston Harbor has its own distinctive personality and its own story to tell, and this urban archipelago offers a unique chance to journey into nature and back into time—all within the shadows of the city skyline. So set sail. Pack your imagination and your love of adventure. There's an island out there, waiting for you.

For information about public programming, check online at bostonharborislands .org. See Resources for more information about recreational opportunities on and around the harbor islands.

A Boston Harbor Islands ferry approaches Spectacle Island with Thompson Island in the background.

The Heart of the Harbor

One of the places to explore on Fort Warren.

Georges Island

WITH ITS LABYRINTH OF DIMLY LIT PASSAGEWAYS, underground dungeons, spooky tunnels, and a drawbridge spanning a dry moat, mighty and historic Fort Warren on Georges Island is one of the most visited attractions on the harbor islands. Though it was active from the 1850s through World War II, Fort Warren's most notable role came when it served as a prison for Confederate soldiers and politicians during the Civil War. A visit to Fort Warren, now an important National Historic Landmark, promises a fascinating, hands-on lesson in history and a ghost story worthy of a good campfire.

Originally known as Pemberton Island (after James Pemberton of Hull, who owned and farmed the island in the seventeenth century), it was rechristened Georges Island by 1710. According to some accounts, the island took its new name from Boston merchant John George Jr., who may have owned land on the island and was likely the same merchant who petitioned the Massachusetts legislature to build Boston Light in 1713.

One of Georges Island's first military moments came during the Revolutionary War, when a large earthwork (a fortification made by altering the landscape) was built in 1778 on the eastern side of the island. At the time, the French fleet was anchored in the harbor for repairs, and the earthwork defended it against the British navy, which was still lurking about Boston Harbor even though they had evacuated the city on March 17, 1776.

The British may have lost America during the Revolutionary War, but thirty-odd years later they managed to successfully cripple Boston's commerce with a naval blockade during the War of 1812. As a result, the United States military decided to upgrade its fortifications along the Eastern seaboard, and the federal government acquired the island for coastal defense in 1825. Because of its strategic location at the throat of the Narrows—the city's main shipping channel until the twentieth century—Georges Island was a natural choice as the site for the new fort.

Demilune on Fort Warren.

By 1825, however, heavy erosion and the sale of sand and gravel to passing ships in need of ballast had diminished Georges Island to half of its original size. The first act taken by the federal government after it purchased the island, therefore, was to build a massive seawall to protect it from further disappearing. By 1833, construction on the fort began in earnest. Fort Warren's ingenious (and very European) design was the brainchild of Sylvanus Thayer, an early superintendent of the U.S. Military Academy known as "the Father of West Point." (Around Boston, he is also remembered as the founder of Thayer Academy in Braintree.) Though the fort was neither attacked nor ever required to fire its cannons, Thayer's

design, which incorporated impenetrable oak doors, portcullises, and a tremendous amount of armament, ensured it would have been ready. The fort was named in honor of Dr. Joseph Warren, a patriot hero who died in the Battle of Bunker Hill—though the name was actually transferred from an existing fort on Governor's Island, which eventually vanished from the map when it was incorporated into Logan Airport.

It would take decades for teams of stonemasons, carpenters, blacksmiths, and other laborers to complete this massive construction project, which was constantly plagued by delays in appropriations and a lack of skilled labor (not an entirely unfamiliar saga to present-day Bostonians). When the military originally purchased Georges Island, it was composed of two drumlins, a topography similar to the East Head of Peddocks Island. Though the design of the fort took advantage of the island's landscape by incorporating the two hills into earthwork protection for the fort, some resculpting had to occur. Lowering and moving these hills in order to accommodate the fort was a considerable task, especially since the work was done by hand, using 536 picks and shovels and 406 wheelbarrows. Moving the granite blocks used to build the fort's twelve-foot-thick foundation walls was no easy feat either. Quarried at Cape Ann and Quincy, the granite blocks were unloaded onto carts at the island's dock, pulled uphill by oxen, and lifted into place by large derricks. It took so long to build Fort Warren that by the time the Civil War began, the fort was still not fully functional, and its defensive design was considered virtually obsolete.

Union soldiers stationed at Fort Warren during the early days of the war are credited with composing the lyrics to the famous marching song "John Brown's Body," which was sung to a tune from an old Methodist revivalist hymn that began, "Say, brothers, will you meet us?" According to some accounts, the song may not have been originally composed to honor the "real" John Brown, the famed abolitionist leader who raided Harper's Ferry, but to poke fun at a soldier at Fort Warren who shared the same name. Regardless, the men of the Massachusetts Infantry who trained at Fort Warren carried the song with them into battle, and its popularity quickly spread through the Union ranks. The rhythm and memorable chorus of "John Brown's Body" made it a natural marching song. When Julia Ward Howe heard Union troops singing the song while marching into battle, she was inspired to write an alternative set of lyrics. Those words, combined with the original melody, became an American anthem: "The Battle Hymn of the Republic."

A little more than six months after the first shots were fired at Fort Sumter, the federal government decided to transport Confederate prisoners to Fort Warren, which was under the command of Colonel Justin Dimick. The veteran officer was told to ready the fort for the arrival of 150 prisoners, so he was understandably shocked when, on Halloween in 1861, a boatload of more than eight hundred men docked at the island. Fort Warren was overrun and ill-prepared, which resulted in food rations and prisoners sleeping on floors. A newspaper account from November 1861 reported that when the prisoners arrived at Fort Warren "pity rather than the hatred of the visitors was excited by the sad spectacle." Bostonians responded by donating food, beds, and other supplies to assist the Confederate prisoners, hoping that their proper treatment might inspire equal compassion toward Union prisoners of war. Additionally, these acts of generosity bolstered the moral high ground of abolitionists.

The most prominent prisoners held at Fort Warren were James Mason and John Slidell, who arrived within a month of the first prisoners. The capture of Mason and Slidell, who were dispatched by Confederate president Jefferson Davis to Europe on a diplomatic mission, provoked the international incident now known as the Trent Affair. The pair were intercepted by Union troops and captured aboard the British mail steamer *Trent.* The British, outraged that one of their ships had been boarded by Union troops, put their fleet on notice and demanded that the two Confederate commissioners

The interior of Fort Warren.

Jay Schmidt on Fort Warren

Ever since Jay Schmidt first visited Fort Warren as a young boy in 1957, he was fascinated by the fort and its history. That curiosity spurred him to spend years researching and writing a book on the fort. Jay talks about his first trip to Fort Warren and his favorite story from its rich history.

"My friend's father was a pilot on a Boston fire boat, and they did harbor cruises on Sundays to inspect facilities. He invited my father, my two brothers, and me to go out to Georges Island. I had no idea there was even a fort out there. At that time, it was in disrepair. The parade ground had not been mown in years—the grass was three feet high—and every room we went into had broken-down timbers and piles of lumber all over the floor. But I was fascinated by the fort and by the stories the caretaker told us. He mentioned Mason and Slidell, and we had just studied them in school. We had such a good time running around the fort and ever since then, I've always been interested in what went on there.

"My favorite story about Fort Warren is the one about the four Confederate prisoners who escaped in 1863 near the sallyport. They slipped out through one of the musketry loopholes and went up and over the coverface. But it turns out the night was too windy and rough to swim off the island, so they had to go back inside the fort, climbing up a rope they had left hanging from the loophole. They waited a couple of nights for the weather to clear, and they escaped again. Two of them were captured in the bushes, but the other two successfully sailed over to Lovells on a large pine board target. The ones who escaped were eventually captured by a revenue cutter near Portland, Maine, and returned to the fort."

be released from Fort Warren. President Abraham Lincoln feared a rift with the British and eventually acquiesced, releasing Mason and Slidell on New Year's Day in 1862.

Other notable Confederate figures detained at Fort Warren were former Kentucky Governor Charles Morehead, Baltimore Mayor George William Brown, General Simon Bolivar Buckner, and Alexander Hamilton Stephens, the vice president of the Confederacy. While life for the prisoners varied depending on their status, rank, and wealth, conditions were never that severe. Indeed, many prisoners praised Dimick for his kindness and humane treatment. When the orders came in March 1862 to direct Buckner to

Fort Warren exterior.

solitary confinement, Dimick was reportedly so distressed that he wept while conveying the order—and was ultimately consoled by Buckner himself, a Confederate general! Dimick garnered so much respect that both Union and Confederate officers served as pallbearers at his funeral in 1871.

Wealthier political prisoners and officers were allowed to supply themselves with whatever luxuries they could afford and make arrangements to buy. More regulations were enforced as the war went on, but in its infancy, prisoners were allowed to receive newspapers, letters, gifts, and even alcohol. When weather permitted, they were allowed outside the doors of their quarters to congregate, walk, or have a smoke.

The main entrance to Fort Warren.

Only thirteen Confederate prisoners out of the hundreds and hundreds who passed through the gates of Fort Warren died on the island, and none were killed by Union troops. In fact, the only recorded executions that occurred on Fort Warren were of two deserters from the Union army: Charles Carpenter and Matthew Riley, "bounty jumpers" who would repeatedly enlist in units to collect a cash bounty, desert, and then join another unit under an assumed name to collect another bounty. They were captured, convicted by a court-martial, and executed by a military firing squad on April 22, 1864.

Of course, if you were to ask anyone familiar with Georges Island what its most enduring story is, they would respond by telling you about The "Lady in Black." Popularized by author and historian Edward Rowe Snow, this tale is now an essential part of the island's fabric.

According to the legend, the wife of a Confederate prisoner, dressed as a man and brandishing a pistol, snuck into the fort in an attempt to free her newlywed husband. She succeeded in reaching her husband's cell, but as they tried to escape the dungeon, Union troops discovered their scheme and notified Colonel Dimick. When the colonel came upon the pair, the wife fired at Dimick, but her gun exploded and killed her husband instead. Dimick had no choice but to order the woman to hang as a spy. Before her execution, she requested that she be properly dressed in women's clothing. She was given black robes and hanged from the gallows.

From the Civil War through World War II, many a soldier stationed on the parapets claimed to see the frightening ghost of the Lady in Black, who is said to prowl through the fort's many passageways to this day. As far back as January 1862, the *Gloucester Telegraph* reported that sentinels keeping midnight rounds saw a spiritual phenomenon near some of the rebel graves. The soldiers reported spying the image of an old woman "vindictively frisking about the ruins of an old building from which she was ejected some time previous to her death." Whether or not Georges Island has a resident ghost is hard to verify, of course, but one thing is for certain—a possible sighting of the Lady in Black was as good an excuse as any when it came to getting out of a monotonous night of guard duty.

The fort remained active through the Spanish-American War, World War I, and World War II, and was increasingly fortified with more powerful guns. During the world wars, Fort Warren was used to monitor and control the mines planted in the southern part of Boston Harbor. After World War II, and with the onset of the atomic age, Fort Warren was rendered militarily

The visitor center and food pavilion at the Georges Island dock.

useless, abandoned, and taken over by the state of Massachusetts. Georges Island was considered as the location for a toxic waste dump in the 1950s, but thanks in part to the efforts of Edward Rowe Snow, those plans were thwarted. Today, a memorial to Snow graces the island he helped to popularize and save, and a shade shelter bears his name.

Georges Island's scenic picnic grounds, open fields, and gravel beach draw as many visitors as Fort Warren itself. Along with Spectacle Island, fifty-three-acre Georges Island is the most-visited island in the harbor chain. It is a forty-five-minute ferry ride from Long Wharf in Boston, and visitors can transfer there for inter-island ferry service to Spectacle, Lovells, Peddocks, Grape, and Bumpkin Islands.

Throughout the summer, Georges Island offers a wide variety of public programs such as Civil War encampments and old-time baseball games. Guided tours of Fort Warren are available daily, and a visitor center brings the history of Fort Warren, its prisoners and enlisted men, and Boston's coastal defenses to life with interactive exhibits and a short film. Don't miss the exhibit that shows what prisoners and soldiers ate at Fort Warren during the Civil War. You might be surprised to learn that many Confederate prisoners dined much more sumptuously than Union enlisted men. If the display makes you hungry, pick up something to eat at the seasonal snack bar under the covered pavilion that sports views of the Boston skyline. Kids can soak up the sun in the adjacent playground that features slides and a replica of Fort Warren.

A pathway leading up from the dock goes by the fort's guard house, underneath a tunnel in the coverface, and to the sallyport. A wooden bridge across the dry moat leads visitors through the fort's original oak doors. The expansive parade ground unfolds as you pass through the sallyport. This field provided space for infantry training and inspections as well as off-duty activities such as baseball games. During wartime, the parade ground was used for temporary support buildings and tents to house additional troops. A granite powder magazine is the only permanent building on the parade ground.

Staircases lead to the grass-covered ramparts, which offer great views of Boston and the neighboring islands. The emplacements for the fort's massive guns can still be seen along the ramparts. The two biggest guns, twelve-inch rifles on disappearing carriages, were located in Battery Stevenson, which was completed in 1902.

Ground-level bastions, filled with dramatic arches and vaulted roofs, will thrill photographers. Visitors can walk through the fort's old bakery, living quarters, and hospital. During the summer, beams of light stream through the narrow musket loops onto the brick walls and wood floors. Children especially love to explore the fort's nooks, crannies, and winding corridors—but keep an eye on them, as some areas have steep drop-offs and hidden hazards.

Toward the end of the day, as the shadows grow long and the sun sinks over Boston, the throngs of visitors to Fort Warren begin to leave on the ferries and the atmosphere of this impressive citadel changes. Soon, you may be all alone. The hallways in front of you begin to fade into the gloaming. The wind begins to howl and the floors creak. A pigeon's flapping wings echo through the empty chambers, and a startling shiver will run down your spine. All around you, the history and legends of Fort Warren coalesce. But if you pay attention, you just might catch a glimpse of something—or someone—from the corner of your eye.

ADDITIONAL INFORMATION

 Family events and history-themed programs are scheduled on summer weekends. For more information, visit bostonharborislands.org.

 Rangers lead guided tours of Fort Warren, including special tours about the legend of the Lady in Black.

 Reservations for day and overnight use of public moorings off Georges Island can be made through Dockwa at dockwa.com or through the Dockwa app. Private boaters may use the dock at Georges Island for passenger pick-up and drop-off only. Dinghies are available for public use. For more information, visit bostonharborislands.org/boating.

 At the time of publication, daily ferries to Georges Island depart from Long Wharf in Boston and the Hingham Shipyard between mid-May and Columbus Day. Inter-island ferries connect to Spectacle, Peddocks, Lovells, Grape, and Bumpkin Islands between late June and Labor Day. For ferry schedule, visit bostonharborislands.org.

A sandy beach draws visitors to
Spectacle Island.

Spectacle Island

THE VIEW FROM THE GRASSY SUMMIT of the north drumlin of Spectacle Island is itself a spectacle to behold. All of metropolitan Boston unfolds before you in a breathtaking, unobstructed 360-degree panorama. Castle Island and Pleasure Bay in South Boston appear as though they are right beneath your feet. And even though the Prudential Tower is over five miles away, it seems as though you could reach out and pluck it from the city skyline. From this vantage point the harbor activity is astonishing. Each sailboat, tanker, tug, and motorboat proclaims the vitality of this maritime city.

Now, turn to the other side of this 157-foot-high perch, where the constellation of islands is perfectly laid out across the shimmering surface of the harbor. In the foreground, Thompson, Long, and Moon Islands stretch across the water. Beyond Long Island, Boston Light is perfectly framed by Gallops and Lovells. And in the distance, the Brewsters point the way toward the open sea. On clear days, you can see up the coast forty miles to the north. This is the highest point in Boston Harbor—a good sixty-eight feet higher than Boston Light.

Fog drapes the Boston skyline as seen from Spectacle Island.

Such a majestic view is a fitting crown for this jewel in the harbor's island necklace. To take in this vista today is to overlook the fact that you are standing atop eighty feet of trash and a legacy of environmental neglect that, unfortunately, was typical of the way Bostonians long treated their harbor and its islands. For decades, Spectacle Island was a wasteland, home to a variety of sordid functions, including a city landfill, horse-rendering factory, and quarantine station.

Now, after nearly fifteen years of environmental cleanup and a cost of more than $170 million, Spectacle Island has been transformed into a 114-acre recreation area, the showpiece of the Boston Harbor Islands national park area. Opened in 2006, the reborn island park includes five miles of walking trails, a marina, swimming beaches, fishing, and an environmentally friendly visitor center. The remarkable renewal of Spectacle Island from a smoldering dump to a public park is representative of the rebirth of the Boston Harbor Islands as a whole.

Formed when glaciers left behind deposits of sand, gravel, rubble, and debris, Spectacle Island has been a "dumping ground" from the beginning. Those deposits produced the island's two drumlins, which the Massachusett tribe, who summered there for thousands of years, referred to as "The Twins." Archaeologists have excavated middens—piles of clam shells and

Visitors walk up the north drumlin of Spectacle Island.

A ranger leads visitors on tour of the summit of Spectacle Island's north drumlin.

other refuse discarded by Native Americans—that date back 1,500 years. Other artifacts found by archaeologists include pottery shards, stone arrowheads, and tools.

When the first European settlers arrived, the two drumlins of the island were connected by a sandbar so narrow that it was submerged by large tidal surges. The colonists came to call this place Spectacle Island because its shape resembled that of a pair of eyeglasses. The Massachusetts Bay Colony granted Spectacle Island—along with Deer, Hog, and Long Islands—to the town of Boston in the 1630s. The yearly rent for all four islands was a total of four shillings. The town rented the land for sixpence an acre to pay for free schools in the new settlement, and the Puritans used the island to graze cattle and harvest lumber for firewood and shipbuilding.

In 1717, Spectacle Island became a makeshift quarantine station "for the reception and entertainment of sick persons coming from beyond the sea, in order to prevent the spreading of infection." The quarantine station was often used for early Irish immigrants thought to be carrying smallpox, measles, or other contagious diseases. Twenty years after the quarantine station was established on Spectacle Island, it was moved to Rainsford Island, and land use returned to agriculture.

By the 1840s, yachtsmen and Bostonians on pleasure excursions discovered the island anew. Vacationers in search of fun flocked to the two summer resorts that opened on the island. It appears, however, that the fun might have been a touch too lively for some. One Sunday in 1856, police arrested a party of about twenty-five men disembarking at Long Wharf after a boat trip to Spectacle Island. The authorities seized a roulette table, cards, and dice and charged these wayward gentlemen with gambling on the boat and the island. Apparently, such nefarious boat trips had become too popular a pastime for a city founded by Puritans, particularly on the Sabbath. Shortly after the police crackdown, the island's hotels ceased operation.

With the resorts gone, Spectacle Island was sold in 1857 to Boston businessman Nahum Ward, who moved his industrial operations offshore to the island. Over the next one hundred years, Ward's factories and the subsequent uses of the island would plague surrounding communities with noxious odors that were often far stronger than the salty ocean breeze. Among the plants built by N. Ward & Co. on the island was a horse-rendering operation. In reality, this was a small—albeit colorful—part of Ward's overall operations, staffed by three or four men out of the sixty he employed, but it was this aspect of Ward's business that earned the island the nickname "Boney Wards."

Spectacle Island offers five miles of walking trails.

As unpalatable as it may seem by today's standards, Ward's disposal of two thousand or more dead horses a year was a necessary evil that helped prevent a public health epidemic in Boston. The company's horse hearses were familiar sights passing along the city streets of Boston, collecting carcasses free of charge. Prior to Ward's company, which was established in 1828, the custom was to throw the dead horses directly into the harbor. Occasionally, the horses were towed out into the open sea only to float back in, becoming entangled in the fingers of the city's wharves or washing onto the shores of the harbor islands.

Once collected, the carcasses were then taken to Ward's wharf where workers sheared and placed the manes in a loft to dry. The hair was steamed, cleansed, and curled for use as mattress and furniture stuffing. Each evening a barge with the horses sailed to Spectacle Island. At the

Though unpalatable, Nahum Ward's horse-rendering plant provided a vital service to the city of Boston, as this 1906 photograph of the produce center in Faneuil Hall demonstrates. *Courtesy of the Library of Congress.*

Visitors wander along Spectacle Island's sandy beaches.

factory, the skins were removed, salted, and prepared for sale to manufacturers of fine upholstery and high-end shoemakers. One year, all the skins were used to make baseballs, perhaps an early indication of Boston's sporting obsession. From the remaining carcasses the factory extracted oils and produced fertilizer. And, yes, the hooves were used for glue. The factory also took in twenty to thirty tons of beef scraps each day. These scraps were pressed into cakes, mixed with other ingredients, and eventually made into dog biscuits. (Distressingly, before the Civil War, the cakes were used to feed slaves as well.) Thankfully, all that remains of Ward's Spectacle Island operations today are the four granite piers at the base of the north drumlin.

Given the unpleasant nature of Ward's business, it's hard to imagine that his employees actually lived on the island. Upwards of fifteen of those employees raised their families there, too. (Families continued to live on Spectacle well into the 1950s.) Perhaps even harder to imagine is that many of the children raised on Spectacle Island considered it paradise. For them, the island provided the wonderful adventure of rural life in clear sight of the city's skyline.

To educate the children of Spectacle Island, the city of Boston established its smallest school. This simple, red, one-room structure could have been ripped from the pages of *Little House on the Prairie*—except that it was located on an island of factories right off the shore of an urban metropolis. The children attended the school until the eighth grade when they were either sent to schools in Boston or put to work on the island. The factory provided the building and furniture, while the city paid for books, stationery, and a teacher, who either stayed on the island while school was in session or traveled to the island daily by towboat.

Ward's factories caused a powerful stench, but residents downwind of Spectacle Island found little relief after the operations closed. In the early 1900s Spectacle Island became home to a grease reclamation facility and disposal plant that converted garbage into various marketable byproducts such as soap and fertilizer. A few years later, the island became a landfill, and the city shipped its garbage there until 1959. By the time the dump closed, the trash was eighty-five feet deep, adding an additional thirty-seven acres to the footprint of Spectacle Island. So deep was the refuse that a bulldozer supposedly sunk into it in the 1950s, never to be found again.

The garbage dump assaulted the senses. Spontaneous methane combustions commonly lit up the night sky. Depending on the wind, the overwhelming smell could be detected at the Farm School on Thompson Island, the City Point section of South Boston, Winthrop, and even as far north as Swampscott. The odor was particularly pungent during the summer, forcing residents to shutter their windows on the hottest and most oppressive days of the year. It is said that the smell was so bad that in foggy weather ships could get their bearings simply by the direction of the stench emanating from Spectacle Island.

In the same year the dump closed, Spectacle Island became the backdrop for another sordid tale—this time a murder

This photograph, taken in 1909 South Boston, demonstrates the disregard with which Boston's waterfront was treated over the years. *Courtesy of the Library of Congress.*

mystery followed by a sensational trial that captured the attention of the United States and the world. In September 1959, a tugboat captain discovered the beaten body of twenty-three-year-old divorcee Lynn Kauffman washed up on the island's shore, clad only in Bermuda shorts and blue slippers. Kauffman had been aboard the Dutch passenger freighter *Utrecht* that had just completed a forty-four-day voyage from Singapore and was sailing to New York City. The ship's handsome (and married) radio officer, Willem van Rie, had been carrying on a torrid affair with Kauffman and, following twenty hours of questioning, admitted to striking her the night of her disappearance. Even though he immediately recanted, police charged him with murder.

Spectacle Island offers five miles of walking trails.

The radio officer stood trial in Suffolk Superior Court in Boston, and van Rie took to the stand in his own defense, proclaiming his innocence. There was no sign of violence in Kauffman's cabin, and witnesses testified that they heard Kauffman in her cabin at seven o'clock the night of her disappearance, at which point the ship was seven or eight miles distant from Spectacle Island. The harbormaster testified that the current could not possibly have swept Kauffman onto the island from that far offshore. The jury acquitted van Rie, and the mystery was never solved. Were the witnesses mistaken? Had she committed suicide? Did she accidentally fall overboard? Or did van Rie—or another passenger—get away with murder?

The media spotlight eventually faded, but Spectacle's squalid conditions persisted far longer. For decades after the landfill closed, Spectacle Island

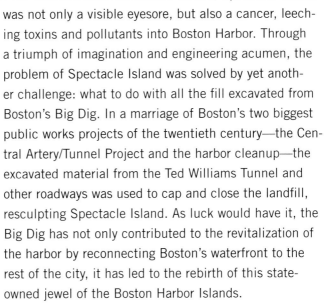
was not only a visible eyesore, but also a cancer, leeching toxins and pollutants into Boston Harbor. Through a triumph of imagination and engineering acumen, the problem of Spectacle Island was solved by yet another challenge: what to do with all the fill excavated from Boston's Big Dig. In a marriage of Boston's two biggest public works projects of the twentieth century—the Central Artery/Tunnel Project and the harbor cleanup—the excavated material from the Ted Williams Tunnel and other roadways was used to cap and close the landfill, resculpting Spectacle Island. As luck would have it, the Big Dig has not only contributed to the revitalization of the harbor by reconnecting Boston's waterfront to the rest of the city, it has led to the rebirth of this state-owned jewel of the Boston Harbor Islands.

In many ways, the project was a throwback to Boston's centuries-old practice of adding fill to its rivers and harbor to expand its footprint and create new neighborhoods, such as the Back Bay. The first barge load of excavated material made the trip to Spectacle Island in 1992. Over the next five years, barge after barge made that same journey, eventually transporting 3.5 million cubic yards of clay, dirt, dredged material, and gravel that would smother the landfill under countless tons of mud. So much fill was added that both drumlins increased by sixty feet in height.

Once the landfill was closed, two to five feet of topsoil were added, and 2,400 trees and 26,000 shrubs were planted. Native and non-native species that thrive in sandy soil, salty air, and harsh wind and sun were chosen. No deep-rooted species that might pierce the cap were planted. Meadow grasses on the sides of the drumlins help maintain the stability of the slopes and dominate the landscape, at least until the deciduous and evergreen trees mature. Vents sprinkled across the island allow methane underneath the ground to escape safely, and the landfill cap is constantly monitored to ensure it is intact. A seawall fourteen feet thick helps prevent the seepage of toxins into the harbor and protects the coastline against erosion.

It is a wonderful quirk of fate that what used to be the most environmentally degraded island in Boston Harbor is now its most environmentally friendly. (Although it should be noted that Spectacle Island displays a tradition of recycling, from the horse-rendering operations to the grease reclamation plant to the use of Big Dig leftovers.) The benches and picnic tables on Spectacle Island are made from recycled materials. Solar panels resting

The view from Spectacle Island's south drumlin.

on the south-facing roof of the visitor center supply enough power for the center and the island's small fleet of electrical vehicles. Water used in the center's kitchen and sinks is collected, filtered, and used to irrigate flowers.

Spectacle Island and the Big Dig

The restoration of Spectacle Island using excavated material from the Big Dig was an extraordinary feat of engineering. The tricky logistics of converting an abandoned landfill into a park were made even more extreme by the landfill's island location. Ron Killian, Chris Barnett, and Ralph DeGregorio of the Central Artery/Tunnel Project give some insight into the complexities of this massive project.

"The entire Spectacle Island project was highly unusual. Landfills that do get restored are not usually islands, so the biggest challenge we faced was building by water. Everything on that island needed to get there by boat—including 3.5 million cubic yards of fill. We had to have a dedicated boating facility on the South Boston side. We had to have barges. We had to have tugs on standby. And all the labor needed to be transported to the island. It was a huge operation. Plus, we had to work under additional environmental requirements and permitting commitments because the site was in the middle of the harbor.

"Virtually no blade of grass was on the island before restoration started. We had to completely wipe the slate clean and rebuild from scratch. And that's something that doesn't hit you when you visit the island today. We built beaches around a third of the perimeter of the island. When we started the project, the 'beaches' on Spectacle were basically eroding trash. We dredged everything up, and put down stone and sand, so the beach you see today is almost completely artificial.

"There was a lot of thought given to the landscaping of the island. We were concerned about sustainability. We selected species for wind, salt, and drought tolerance. And, of course, we were concerned with resistance to disease. We didn't want the island to be a monoculture that could be wiped out by one bug. We also looked at animal habitats and what shrubbery would provide cover and food for birds. We wanted tree species that weren't going to topple, as the soil doesn't have much depth to it because it's a landfill cap.

"The same consideration was given to the seawalls. When people go around the island they say: "These are some seawalls! What were they thinking?" And what we were thinking was a storm surge, high tides, and waves."

The north drumlin of Spectacle Island.

There are modern composting toilets that use no water or chemicals. By all accounts, Spectacle Island is authentically *green*.

As one of the hub islands, and just thirty minutes from downtown Boston, Spectacle Island offers a wide array of recreational opportunities not to be missed. Sand was imported to create a popular swimming beach complete with rinse stations and changing facilities. The marina is available to private boaters on a first-come, first-served basis, and moorings are located on the north side of the main pier. And lest you think Spectacle offers nothing but lazy days on the beach, summertime brings Sunday jazz concerts, guided tours, kayak expeditions, yoga classes, and a slew of public programming for children. Birders can spot upward of one hundred different species, such as bobolinks, warblers, Savannah sparrows, and even wild turkeys; and anglers, who are often seen at the end of the dock, say the stripers, cod, and flounder are among the fish biting.

Be sure to pack sunblock as there are few natural shaded areas. The walking trails on Spectacle Island provide both easy strolls, such as the 1.8-mile perimeter trail, and vigorous climbs. Gravel pathways carved into the north and south drumlins wind their ways to the summits. Atop the peaks are picnic areas and charming gazebos. Wayfaring signs include historical vignettes about the island's past, and, in the late summer and early fall, migrating monarch butterflies flutter among the wildflowers along the trails.

Stroll the beach after a storm, and you'll discover a bounty of colorful sea glass and earthenware shards amid the blue mussel and common slipper shells. The park asks visitors not to harvest the relics, but to leave them on the island for others to enjoy as well.

Sea glass and earthenware shards are common sights on Spectacle Island's shoreline.

During the summer, a snack bar is open in the visitor center, and the island hosts popular Thursday night sunset clambakes prepared by local celebrity chefs. The visitor center also has restrooms and exhibits about island history, but the best part is outside, under the porch. There, a long row of Adirondack chairs look out on the harbor and city skyline. If you happen to find yourself relaxing in one of those chairs during a concert, you'll discover that the sense of renewal exuded by this revitalized island can reach into a visitor's soul.

ADDITIONAL INFORMATION

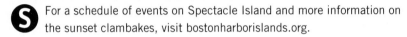 For a schedule of events on Spectacle Island and more information on the sunset clambakes, visit bostonharborislands.org.

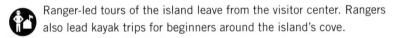 Ranger-led tours of the island leave from the visitor center. Rangers also lead kayak trips for beginners around the island's cove.

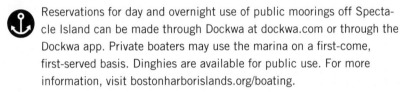 Reservations for day and overnight use of public moorings off Spectacle Island can be made through Dockwa at dockwa.com or through the Dockwa app. Private boaters may use the marina on a first-come, first-served basis. Dinghies are available for public use. For more information, visit bostonharborislands.org/boating.

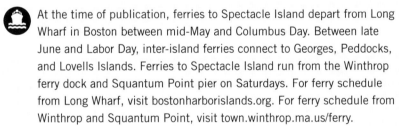 At the time of publication, ferries to Spectacle Island depart from Long Wharf in Boston between mid-May and Columbus Day. Between late June and Labor Day, inter-island ferries connect to Georges, Peddocks, and Lovells Islands. Ferries to Spectacle Island run from the Winthrop ferry dock and Squantum Point pier on Saturdays. For ferry schedule from Long Wharf, visit bostonharborislands.org. For ferry schedule from Winthrop and Squantum Point, visit town.winthrop.ma.us/ferry.

The visitor center at Spectacle Island features exhibits, restrooms, and a snack bar.

A shaded picnic ground with incredible
views on Lovells Island.

Lovells Island

FROM THE SOUTHERN BEACH OF LOVELLS ISLAND, the shoreline of Georges Island seems so close it's hard to imagine that for centuries the waterway between them was the lone shipping lane into Boston. Particularly at low tide, it's easy to see how deadly shipwrecks on Lovells Island were once fairly common occurrences. The Narrows, as it's known, is a rocky passage, only a quarter mile from shore to shore and with a channel no more than two hundred yards wide. For large ships and big ocean steamers making their way to Boston's port, the trip by Lovells Island was no easier than threading a needle.

If you think driving the narrow, crooked streets of downtown Boston is hair-raising, consider plotting a course through its harbor: The islands that bless Boston Harbor were (and can be) a curse to negotiate even under the best conditions. Before the modern-day benefits of GPS and detailed nautical charts, captains were forced to contend with hidden shoals, powerful currents, and the sheer volume of sailing vessels. The names of harbor landmarks—Hypocrite Channel, Devil's Back, and the Roaring Bulls—in no way belie the peril that faced ships in the final ten miles of their journey. Tiptoeing through the precarious approach to reach the safety of the deep inner harbor was tricky enough for experienced pilots, let alone for those seeing it for the first time.

The real danger came from unpredictable weather that could quickly transform conditions from placid to fierce. Many a boat has been lost in the fog or blown ashore by a howling nor'easter. During the winter, frozen sea spray could encrust a ship in ice, making it impossible to work the sails. The skeletons of hundreds of ships that litter the floor of Boston Harbor testify to its difficult passage.

A number of these ships met their end on Lovells Island, in plain sight of the city. How terrifying it must have been for those survivors shipwrecked on Lovells, particularly during the winter when they had to endure bitter winds through the darkness of night. And how frustrating it must have been to be so close to safety—with the

A sign on an old battery on Fort Standish.

warm, alabaster glow of Boston in the distance—but too far for anyone to
know they were there.

One of the most notable shipwrecks on Lovells Island was that of the
seventy-four-gun French warship *Magnifique.* In 1782, during the waning
days of the Revolutionary War, the ship ran aground on the western side of
the island while trying to navigate the Narrows. Although he may have been
a bit of a scapegoat, David Darling, the Boston pilot of the *Magnifique,*
never lived down the mistake. He later became a church sexton and an
undertaker—fitting, perhaps, for someone who sent a ship to its watery
grave. It is said that neighborhood children would rib Darling by chalking
the church doors with the lines, "Don't you run this ship ashore, as you did
the seventy-four!"

Darling's error and the subsequent wreck had considerable implications
for American history. Fearing a rift with their major ally, the Americans presented France with the seventy-four-gun USS *America* as compensation—
even though the vessel had been promised to naval hero John Paul Jones,
who'd diligently supervised its construction. Without an American ship to
command, the Father of the American Navy traveled to France and eventually

entered into the service of the Russian navy under Catherine the Great. To this day, treasure hunters continue to be lured to the shoals of Lovells Island by the dream of recovering the gold and silver coins said to be aboard the *Magnifique.*

Four years after the *Magnifique* wrecked, a tragic fate befell a packet ship from Maine. One dark December night during a blizzard, the ship ran aground on the rocks of Ram's Head, a bar extending off the northern side of the island. All thirteen passengers and crew managed to make it to shore, but the elements were simply too harsh. Without shelter, the survivors eventually died of exposure. When found the following morning, it is said that a young couple engaged to be married was found dead in each other's arms,

A remnant of Fort Standish's lookout tower.

The remnants of a gun battery on Lovells Island.

huddled behind a boulder in their desperate quest for survival. The rock, located on the western side of the island, was dubbed "Lovers' Rock."

The author of the first American bestseller, Susanna Rowson, was aboard yet another ship that wrecked on Lovells Island. In January 1767, four-year-old Rowson was traveling with her father, a British revenue officer transferring to the port of Boston. The ship ran aground at night, and the sea encased it in ice. Luckily, everyone on board was saved by fishermen living on Lovells. Twenty-three years later, Rowson wrote the novel *Charlotte Temple,* the biggest-selling book in the United States until *Uncle Tom's Cabin*; but Rowson's subsequent book, *Rebecca*, drew from her horrific experience on Lovells Island.

The spate of shipwrecks off Lovells Island led to the construction of the first hut of refuge in the United States by the Massachusetts Humane Society in 1787. The small red hut on the Narrows side of the island offered salvation in the form of dry clothing, food, blankets, wood, and a flint and tinder to kindle a fire. No sooner had the hut been built than it was credited with saving the lives of six people whose shallop bound for Cape Ann wrecked off Lovells' coast. A similar hut was built on the east end of Lovells in 1789. Scores of comparable structures arose along the Massachusetts coast in following years, and the hut was part of the first organized

The ruins of the oil house that once served the range lights on Lovells Island.

lifesaving efforts in North America and a precursor of the U.S. Coast Guard. The frequent shipwrecks in Boston Harbor also gave rise to a proud tradition of lifesaving among brave volunteers from Hull who saved hundreds of people from distressed ships.

At the turn of the twentieth century a second entrance to Boston Harbor was dredged through Broad Sound, and a pair of range lights constructed

A former gun battery now has a picnic table on Lovells Island.

on Lovells Island guided mariners through the new shipping channel. The range lights, located on the northern side of the island, stood until they were torn down in 1939 so that the military could use the land as a rifle range. The only surviving structure from the range lights is the dilapidated shell of the little, redbrick oil house, which stored the fuel that lit the beacons. (The Friends of the Boston Harbor Islands is working with the Massachusetts Department of Conservation and Recreation and National Park Service to save and restore the historic oil house.)

Now the primary entrance for deep-draft ships, the channel through Broad Sound increased the strategic importance of Lovells Island, as the harbor's two principal openings flanked the island. As a result, the federal government in 1900 added the island to the growing list of military sites peppering the harbor. Named in honor of the Pilgrim Miles Standish, Fort Standish served Boston from the Spanish-American War all the way through World War II. Although Fort Standish was only a lightly manned sub-post of Fort Warren during the Spanish-American War, it was fully garrisoned in World War I. Between the world wars, Fort Standish was placed on caretaker status, but it was reactivated for World War II, at which time it had sixty structures.

Gazing out on Lovells Island.

The numerous ruins of Fort Standish, abandoned in the late 1940s, are sure to delight those interested in military history. Most striking are the hulking gun batteries. Though they are now crumbling and obsolete, these batteries, along with the cracking asphalt roads, stand testament to the island's days as a military installation. Today, these roads have been reinvented as hiking trails, and the walk along the east side of the island leads to Battery Burbeck-Morris. This towering battery emerges suddenly, and the concrete staircase leading to the top of the battery has the desolate feel of an Aztec temple.

Cut into the island's central drumlin, Battery Burbeck-Morris once held ten-inch rifles with a range of nine miles, firing over earthen parapets before recoiling out of sight. The guns were dismounted in 1943, and the parapets long ago surrendered to an invasion of staghorn sumacs. (Some staircases to the top of the battery lack railings, so explorers should use caution.)

Walking counterclockwise around Lovells Island, the trail north of Battery Burbeck-Morris ends amid white sand dunes and wispy grasses. Continuing north along the shore of Broad Sound, the island begins to narrow. The area surrounding the oil house is carpeted with mussel shells, washed ashore from the flats of Broad Sound. North of the oil house is a salt marsh and

Staghorn sumac on Lovells Island.

heavily wooded area that is more difficult to traverse. At the northern tip of Lovells Island are the remains of Battery Terrill.

If the east side of the island has you thinking you've discovered Aztec ruins, the west side of the island will give you a more apocalyptic feel, eerily reminiscent to the finale of *Planet of the Apes.* The beach leads past the ruins of massive searchlight platforms that have collapsed from the eroding bluff above. Near the old dock, enormous pieces of rubble from the fort's World War I compound are partially exposed.

Continue south toward the present-day pier, and you'll come across a long stretch of sand dunes and staghorn sumac groves. Near the pier is the remnant of a lookout tower perched on four concrete pillars. Through the narrow lookout slot, military men once took measurements to help aim gun and mortar batteries.

Berries on Lovells Island.

Campsites for both groups and individuals are scattered across Lovells Island—though one of the most unique settings has to be on the south side of the island, in the old parade grounds. During the summer the parade grounds are filled with tents, hemmed in by the concrete ruins of Battery Whipple and Battery Williams. Battery Whipple held two six-inch guns with a range of nine miles. Battery Williams, built in the early 1900s, mounted three-inch rapid fire guns with a range of just over five miles to protect both the Narrows and Broad Sound from possible attack. The emplacements below housed officer and gun crew day rooms, an equipment storehouse, and magazines.

Behind the two batteries on the island's southeastern tip, tidal pools teeming with sea-life thrive amid the remnants of the old seawall. It takes a little effort to scale the large stones, but it provides a great location to watch the gulls scouting the pools for their next meal. It also offers a superb view of Boston Light on Little Brewster Island, the towering bluff on Great Brewster Island, Graves Light, and the open sea beyond.

Just north of the seawall—and directly across the island from the pier—is a long, sweeping beach that curves along Broad Sound. If you're planning to take a dip, the water in the Broad Sound is far more suitable for swimming than the swiftly moving currents along the Narrows; however, the beach along Broad Sound is rocky and not staffed by lifeguards.

While Spectacle Island is a better option for swimming, camping on Lovells is still popular due to its proximity to the city. The foghorns, planes, and party boats have been known to make the island a noisy choice, but it's all worth it for the opportunity to relax on a beach and watch the sunset over the Boston skyline.

ADDITIONAL INFORMATION

Group and individual campsites are available on Lovells Island. Reservations are required and can be made online at ReserveAmerica .com or by calling toll-free (877) 422-6762. At the time of publication, reservations cost $8 for Massachusetts residents and $10 for non-residents and are available daily from late June to early September. Campgrounds have composting toilets, picnic tables, and nearby charcoal grills but there is no on-island running water, electricity, or concessions. Campgrounds are in high demand, so make reservations early. Reservations are taken as much as six months in advance. For campground availability, call (617) 223-8666.

For boaters arriving by private craft, docks are for passenger pick-up and drop-off only.

At the time of publication, ferries to Lovells Island run from late June to Labor Day. To get to Lovells Island from Long Wharf, take the free inter-island ferry from Georges Island. An inter-island ferry also connects to the Hingham Shipyard. For ferry schedule, visit boston harborislands.org.

Gallops Island is closed to the public.

Gallops Island

TUCKED AWAY IN THE NORTH END'S LANGONE PARK, a gray stone pedestal topped by a sinking ship and a band of Morse code stands largely unnoticed. The monument honors the graduates of the Gallops Island Radio Training Station who gave their lives aboard merchant ships supplying American forces during World War II.

This overlooked statue seems to symbolize the forgotten island where it once stood. Closed to the public for years, Gallops Island, which protected Boston from the double threats of disease and attack, has begun to fade from Boston's collective consciousness.

Used by Native Americans for thousands of years, the island takes its name from Captain John Gallop, a noted Boston Harbor pilot who owned it along with Nixes Mate in the 1600s. Gallops Island's fertile land was used for agriculture into the early nineteenth century, and its farms often supplied ships anchored in Nantasket Roads with vegetables and other important staples.

But Gallops Island has a rich and unique military record as well. During the Revolutionary War, French troops protected the harbor by erecting earthen batteries and mounting cannons on the island's northern bluff. During the Civil War, as many as three thousand Union soldiers on their way to and from the warfront were quartered on the island. (Before receiving their final discharge and parading through the streets of Boston, the famed 54th Massachusetts Volunteer Infantry Regiment, immortalized in the film *Glory*, spent a number of days encamped on the island in the summer of 1865.)

After the Civil War, Boston moved its quarantine station from Deer Island to Gallops. Arriving immigrants brought ashore on Gallops Island were forced to strip and scrub themselves with disinfectants. Between 1867 and 1937, hundreds of thousands of immigrants as well as Bostonians believed to be afflicted with yellow fever, smallpox, cholera, and even leprosy were quarantined on the island. At the quarantine station's peak in 1886, medical staff examined fifty thousand patients brought to the island.

Doctors couldn't save every patient. Nearly 250 people remain buried in an unmarked cemetery along the shoreline on the eastern end of the island. With harsh winter storms eroding the cemetery and exposing coffins and remains, the Massachusetts Department of Conservation and Recreation, which owns the twenty-three-acre island, has begun the work of excavating and identifying the dead and stabilizing the site. Remains will be reburied in veterans' cemeteries and a Hyde Park cemetery.

While not the threat it was to colonial Boston, smallpox remained a dire concern for public health officials even at the dawn of the twentieth century. During the smallpox epidemic of May 1901, the city not only isolated the sick on Gallops Island but also offered free vaccinations to the healthy. Because considerable reluctance to vaccinate remained, the city ordered house-to-house inoculations. Anyone who refused paid a $5 fine or served a fifteen-day jail sentence. "Virus squads" were dispatched to rooming houses, where police officers pinned down the homeless so that physicians could administer the vaccine. By the end of 1903, these highly questionable tactics helped to contain the epidemic.

Gallops Island was the site of a showdown between the Board of Health and one of the more vocal opponents of smallpox vaccinations. Dr. Immanuel Pfeiffer—who held that proper diet and cleanliness were the only reasonable means to ward off the disease—requested that he be allowed to visit the smallpox hospital on Gallops Island without the required vaccination. To silence critics, the chairman of Boston's Board of Health agreed. Two weeks after Pfeiffer's visit to the hospital on January 23, 1902, he was found critically ill in his Bedford home. "Sympathy for him is entirely lacking," reported *The Boston Globe*, "and the epithets applied to him are neither mild nor elegant, one of the least suggestive being that he is 'an old chump.'" Pfeiffer survived, and even though he remained stubbornly opposed to vaccination, his ordeal essentially put an end to the debate in Boston.

A little more than a decade later, the country was plunged into World War I. The ink had barely dried on the declaration of war against Germany when on April 6, 1917, American sailors and Boston police boarded and seized German steamers that had found refuge in Boston Harbor when the war in Europe had begun. Nearly three hundred German officers and crew were taken as prisoners of war and imprisoned on Deer Island before being transferred to Gallops Island. Once on Gallops, they tended gardens, built houses, opened small workshops, and even laid out a tennis court.

When World War II broke out, Gallops Island again served in defense of the country. President Franklin D. Roosevelt realized that winning the war would require thousands of ships to carry supplies to the fronts, and the newly established U.S. Maritime Service was charged with training civilian volunteers to operate those vessels. From July 1940 to October 1945, the Radio Training Station on Gallops Island prepared thousands of radio operators, with as many as fifty a week completing the twenty-week training program. Once graduated, these men became the ears of the ship. They were the first to hear warning signals of danger and responsible for tapping out the first calls for help.

The radio school was abandoned after the war. Foundations from some of the buildings remain along with broken concrete paths and the parade ground on the top of the island's drumlin. Ruins from the quarantine hospital also remain, along with fruit trees and flowering shrubs. Unfortunately, Gallops Island was closed in 2000 due to the presence of asbestos-containing debris among the ruins, and it's unclear when the island will reopen.

Perhaps, then, it's just as well that the monument to the Radio Training Station is no longer on the island's shores. While it may seem overshadowed in the North End park, a curious eye will appreciate this well-deserved tribute to the men who lost their lives in service to their country.

ADDITIONAL INFORMATION

 Reservations for day and overnight use of public moorings off Gallops Island can be made through Dockwa at dockwa.com or though the Dockwa app. Private boaters are prohibited from landing on Gallops. For more information, visit bostonharborislands.org/boating.

Nixes Mate with the Boston skyline in the background.

Nixes Mate

JUST NORTH OF GALLOPS ISLAND LIES a simple beacon with a peculiar name—Nixes Mate. The octagonal pyramid, familiar to some as the logo for the Friends of the Boston Harbor Islands, is perched on a mighty square base of granite blocks. The purpose of the black-and-white-striped marker, which is listed on the National Register of Historic Places, is to warn boaters of the dangerous gravel shoal on which it stands—but in a way, it's also a memorial to an island lost to the sea.

It's hard to believe looking at it today, but during the 1600s, Nixes Mate was a twelve-acre island in the heart of Boston Harbor. It was so large that it was used for pasturing sheep. By 1805, when the beacon was erected, all that remained were rocky flats covered at high tide. Where did the island go?

According to one salty yarn, centuries ago a Captain Nix was killed at sea and his mate was charged with the murder. Despite protesting his innocence, Nix's mate was sentenced to death and taken to the island to be hanged. Before his execution, the accused prophesized that the island would be washed away by the angry sea as proof of his innocence. Still another legend has it that Nix was a pirate who sailed into Boston Harbor with a ship laden with treasure. After anchoring near the island, he and his mate went ashore and buried their booty. But according to this account, Captain Nix was unconvinced his mate could keep the secret, so Nix buried him along with the loot.

Not to spoil a good story, but considerably less-thrilling facts hold that over two hundred years of waves and wind whittled the island away, as did the extraction of stone for ballast. And, given that the isle was referred to as Nixes Island as far back as 1636—six years after the Puritans arrived in Boston, when it was granted to John Gallop, the namesake of Gallops Island—the legends seem even more unlikely.

However, Nixes Mate still has a colorful history connected with pirates who lurked along the New England coast, pounced on their unsuspecting prey (even in sight of Outer Brewster Island), and threatened Boston's maritime commerce. In the 1700s, several convicted pirates were executed and then buried on Nixes Mate. One buccaneer met a more ignominious fate. William Fly was a pirate chief who led a mutiny aboard the slave ship *Elizabeth* in 1726, casting the captain and chief mate overboard. Following his capture, he was condemned to death along with two others. According to *The Boston News-Letter* account in its July 14, 1726, issue, "Their bodies were carried in a boat to a small island called Nick's Mate, about two leagues from the town, where Fly was hung up in irons, as a spectacle for the warning of others, especially sea-faring men." Fly's body was suspended on gibbet chains on Nixes Mate like a scarecrow, his flesh plucked to pieces by seabirds until his bare bones rattled in the breeze. Bird Island, now buried somewhere under the runways at Logan Airport, was another harbor island where executed sea robbers were hung in chains as a gruesome warning to mariners considering hoisting the black flag.

While the golden age of piracy ended in the 1730s, sea bandits remained a curse as late as 1832, when Spanish pirates from the *Panda* boarded the *Mexican*, based in Salem, Massachusetts. The pirates robbed the *Mexican* of $20,000 in silver and unsuccessfully attempted to kill the crew by setting fire to the vessel. They were eventually captured, brought to Boston, and sentenced to death. Captain Pedro Gilbert and four accomplices were hanged in front of a crowd of more than 20,000 people on a spring morning in 1835. Apparently, one of the condemned attempted suicide the night before by inflicting a deep gash on the left side of his neck with a piece of tin. He never regained consciousness, but he was still taken to the gallows, seated in a chair, and executed when the trap door opened. The pirates proclaimed their innocence to the end, but—unlike the legendary mate of Captain Nix—they were kind enough not to consign any islands to the bottom of Boston Harbor.

Nixes Mate with Graves Light in the background.

Is There Buried Treasure in Boston Harbor?

Sure, pirates lurked in the waters of the Caribbean, but like many of today's vacationers, bygone buccaneers enjoyed summer in New England, too. During the 1600s and 1700s, sea bandits such as Blackbeard and William Kidd sparked terror among ship captains sailing in and out of Boston.

Treasure hunters have long been fueled by rumors that pirates buried their booty or hid their ill-gotten goods amid the islands of Boston Harbor. If they did, they unfortunately took the whereabouts to their graves. Still, tales surrounding the lost treasure of the infamous Captain Kidd, arrested in Boston in 1699 before being shipped to London for execution, persist. A letter from Kidd, which turned out to be a forgery, claimed he buried two treasure chests on Governor's Island, now part of Logan Airport. Other stories claim that Kidd hid silver and gold on the coast of Winthrop near Deer Island. Likewise, the pirate "Long Ben" Avery was said to have buried a stash of diamonds on Gallops Island—which, curiously, have yet to be found.

But it's not just pirate tales luring those in search of buried treasure. Hundreds of ships have met an untimely demise among the islands, scattering their contents on the island shores or taking their cargoes to the bottom of the sea. The most notorious wreck was that of the seventy-four-gun French man-of-war *Magnifique*, which was said to have carried gold and silver when it sank off Lovells Island in 1782. Despite evidence that the French crew offloaded its valuable cargo, dreams of finding silver and gold coins still pique the interest of treasure hunters.

So, is there really treasure buried on the islands of Boston Harbor? Aargh! If we knew for sure, do you think we'd tell you?

Captain Kidd and pirates burying treasure on Gardiner's Island in New York, USA (circa late seventeenth century). Vintage etching circa late nineteenth century. *powerofforever/GettyImages*.

The view looking eastward on Rainsford Island.

Rainsford Island

LITTLE CLUES TO THE PAST ARE SCATTERED across Rainsford Island—
reminders left behind by the people who shaped the rich history of
this intriguing island. Like many of the islands in Boston Harbor,
Rainsford housed the more "troublesome" members of Boston's
population. For nearly two centuries, this small isle was home to a
quarantine hospital, almshouse, veterans' house, and boys' reforma-
tory. But Rainsford wasn't all gloom and doom—a thriving summer
resort flourished there as well.

The incoming tide is known to dredge up fragments of these ear-
lier days. For the keen observer, a walk along the beach could yield
a pipe stem, a buffalo nickel, a piece of stoneware, or a belt buckle
of a Civil War veteran. The most vivid reminders of the past, however, are found on the rocky outcrops on the south side of the island.
There, previous islanders meticulously carved their inscriptions into
the slate. Dr. Jerome Van Crowninshield Smith, who became mayor
of Boston in 1854, left his mark: "J.V.C. Smith appointed Physician

Of this Island 1826." Latin inscriptions, such as "Es Deus quia vides omnia negotia—William Kendall, 1835," drive home the point that this isn't your typical graffiti. (Translation: "You are God because you see all business.") One crudely drawn inscription on the rocks may also be the most curious: "1647." If that truly is the year it was made, it was done by one of the earliest European settlers—perhaps by Edward Rainsford himself, the colonist who settled on the island in 1636.

Rainsford, the first ruling elder of the Old South Church, received permission from John Winthrop to raise cattle on the island. Colonists used the island for farming and grazing until 1737, when Rainsford Island replaced Spectacle Island as the site of Boston's quarantine station. From then on, the island was also somberly referred to as "Hospital Island" or "Pest House Island." Though unpleasant, the island served an important function. After the arrival of European settlers, typhoid, yellow fever, and smallpox were highly contagious and lethal diseases that constantly threatened Boston, and the Rainsford Island quarantine station provided a vulnerable population with a critical layer of protection.

Smallpox was a particularly virulent scourge on Boston, and epidemics in Boston were all-too-common occurrences well into the 1800s, with the last major epidemic occurring in Boston as late as 1903. One potent outbreak of the "speckled monster" coincided with the siege of Boston in 1775 and 1776. Indeed, smallpox may have played an even greater role in the American Revolution than it is typically given credit. General George Washington—who was immune from smallpox as he'd survived the disease at the age of nineteen—suspected the British of bioterrorism. In a letter to the Continental Congress on December 4, 1775, he recounted testimony of a sailor claiming that the British had deliberately infected a number of people coming out of Boston "with [the] design of spreading the smallpox through this country and camp." Ten days later, after seeing an increasing number of cases in people leaving Boston, Washington reiterated his suspicion that smallpox was "a weapon of defense they are using against us." While it is impossible to know for certain if the British employed germ warfare, we do know that by 1776 there were more than five thousand reported cases of smallpox, making the patriots somewhat reluctant to return to the city after the British evacuation.

Smallpox epidemics persisted, fueled by the increase in immigration of the mid-1800s. Boats from the West Indies and Europe were the primary vessels carrying pestilence to the city. Physicians would inspect Boston-bound ships before docking at the wharves and quarantine sick passengers and crew. Sometimes boats would anchor off Rainsford Island for days before receiving an all-clear. (The *Beaver*, one of the three ships involved in the Boston Tea Party, spent a week off Rainsford in quarantine until it was released the night before the colonists dumped the tea into the harbor.)

A 1756 law spelled out the procedure for inbound ships: "Inquiry shall be made by the officer on duty at Castle William [Castle Island], of every vessel coming from the sea . . . and if any vessel inquired of as aforesaid shall have any sickness on board, and upon further inquiry the same shall appear to be the plague, smallpox, or any other malignant infectious distemper, in such case shall be given to the master or commander of such vessel to anchor as near the hospital at Rainsford's Island as conveniently may be." Once cleared by the quarantine station at Rainsford, the master of the vessel had twenty-four hours to deliver certificates and flags declaring the vessel free from disease to the health office at Faneuil Hall.

In addition to those arriving by sea, infected Bostonians were sometimes transported to the isolated island. Some of those quarantined on Rainsford Island never left and were laid to rest on the west side of the island. It's been said that those who died of the disease in the city itself were occasionally buried on Rainsford, too. On such occasions, a city employee would row to the mainland under the cover of darkness, absconding back to the island with the potentially infectious body. Hundreds, if not thousands, of people were buried on Rainsford Island. In the 1930s, the bodies were reinterred on Long Island. However, since the workers lacked detailed maps of the burial ground, it's almost certain there are still remains on the island.

Rainsford Island continued to play a vital role in controlling the smallpox epidemics throughout the nineteenth century, and its limited resources were put to the test as the harbor's activity increased. By 1832, it was clear that the smallpox hospital facilities would need to be improved, and a magnificent three-story Greek Revival stone structure was built on a perch on the island's rocky southwest corner. The glorious Stone Hospital would have been a towering sight to those sailing into the harbor. Its soaring white columns, reminiscent of the Parthenon, earned it the nickname of the "Greek Temple."

Strangely enough, Rainsford Island hosted tourists at a summer resort between epidemics. It may not exactly have been Club Med, but the island provided plenty of amusement. The Old Mansion House on the island's eastern bluff, built in 1819, provided summer accommodations in addition to quarters for the island keeper's and resident physician's families. Guests enjoyed the licensed tavern and reading room filled with all the principal newspapers from across the country. When there were no infectious patients about, summer parties overflowed the hospital buildings with guests enjoying copious amounts of chowder and champagne.

The quarantine station was moved to Deer Island in the 1840s, but Rainsford Island continued its institutional missions. It became the site of an almshouse in 1852 and, after the Civil War, a home to veterans of that awful conflict. In 1895, Rainsford Island hosted the House of Reformation, renamed the Suffolk School for Boys in the early twentieth century. Young men between the ages of eight and sixteen were kept busy in the island's print, shoe, and garment shops. One of the harbor's most interesting characters—Portuguese Joe—made his home just off the south coast of

This 1840s oil painting by Robert Salmon depicts both the harbor activity and the Stone Hospital on Rainsford Island. *Rainsford's Island, Boston Harbor. Photograph © the Museum of Fine Arts Boston.*

Ellen Berkland, Massachusetts Department of Conservation and Recreation Archaeologist

The Boston Harbor Islands provide the most unspoiled archaeological sites in the city of Boston. Ellen Berkland explains the archaeological importance of the islands and what to do if you locate an artifact.

"The Boston Harbor Islands have not been impacted or developed to the same extent as the rest of the city, so the potential for finding ancient sites is extremely high. The islands offer us an amazing look at the peopling of New England and Boston over a span of 11,000 years. Native Americans didn't leave any documents, so we're learning about their daily lives and activities through our findings on the islands. Unfortunately, only a small percentage of archaeological sites have been excavated on the islands, and presently wind and rain are eroding these fragile non-renewable cultural resources at an alarming rate.

"The Boston Harbor Islands are part of an archaeological district, and its resources, both below ground and above ground, are protected under federal mandate. If you find an artifact, leave it as you found it for the next person to enjoy. If you believe you have found something significant, note the location, take a photograph, and call the state archaeologist at the Massachusetts Historical Commission. I always tell people to follow the mantra: Take nothing but pictures, and leave nothing but footprints."

The phone number of the state archaeologist is (617) 727-8470.

Archaeologist Ellen Berkland joins photo historian Liz Carella in leading a group on a survey of Rainsford Island.

Rainsford Island, on what is known as Quarantine Rocks. Portuguese Joe was a lobsterman forced off Long Island in the 1890s. While other lobstermen floated their houses to Peddocks Island, Portuguese Joe decided to build on the exposed terrain off Rainsford's shore. He floated out the timber and used dry eelgrass under the floorboards and inside the walls as insulation. Somehow his house and shanties remained upright for forty-odd years. Everyone thought Joe was crazy, but Portuguese Joe's became a harbor landmark and a popular place to buy lobsters, nonetheless.

The Suffolk School for Boys closed in 1920, and the city of Boston failed in its attempt to sell the island. The city burned down the remaining buildings on the island in the 1930s, so little remains of these structures today. The ledge on the southwest part of Rainsford Island where the Greek Temple once surveyed the harbor is now a grassy area. The temple has been reduced to rubble.

Below that perch are the rocky outcrops where island occupants left their inscriptions. (Unfortunately, vandals have used less artistic graffiti to paint over some of these carvings.) In the opposite direction, toward the city skyline, is the site of the cemetery, now overgrown with tall grasses. There are no headstones and, save for a few bollards that presumably supported tabletop tombs, no other evidence of the cemetery remains.

This inscription on Rainsford Island references Dr. Jerome Van Crowninshield Smith, later elected mayor of Boston.

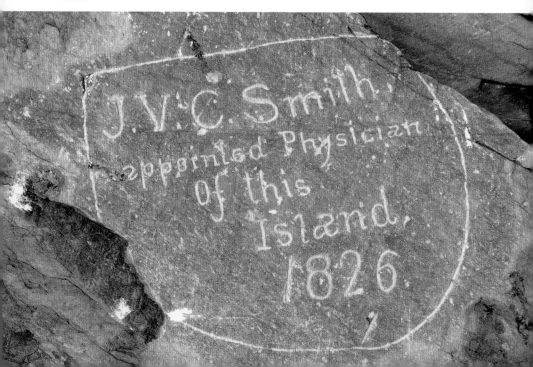

A robust lilac hedge, which harkens back to the nineteenth century when cultivated gardens dotted the landscape, separates the cemetery from the sandbar that connects the two drumlins of Rainsford Island. The isthmus provides a prime spot for kayakers and private boaters to come ashore. (There is no dock or public ferry service to Rainsford Island.)

The eastern drumlin of Rainsford Island, while graded down, still provides the highest lookout on the island at nearly fifty feet. Rainsford does not have maintained hiking trails, so it's a bit of an effort to mount the hill through the brush. Remnants of the apple, plum, and peach orchards, however, do remain. The eastern end, atop an eroding bluff, provides great vistas of Georges and Peddocks Islands. Watch your step for vestiges of the wells and foundations from institutional use of the island.

The twenty-one-acre island is owned and maintained by the city of Boston and is its easternmost point. Camping is not allowed; and, unfortunately, vandals have desecrated some of the historical remnants. However, unvarnished reminders of the past remain on Rainsford Island, and it's a place that sets your imagination loose to ponder centuries of Boston history.

Inscriptions made by previous residents of Rainsford Island are etched into the island's cliffside.

Sherman "Pat" Morss, Jr.

Moon Island

SADLY, MOON ISLAND'S STORY is not as pretty as its name.

For centuries, Boston's sewage was discharged into drains along the streets that emptied into the city's streams and bays. By the 1870s, this rudimentary system posed a considerable threat to public health, and a special commission recommended construction of a new system, which used intercepting sewers, tunnels, and pump stations to transport Boston's sewage to gigantic reservoirs on Moon Island. The four granite lagoons, capable of holding fifty million gallons of raw sewage at a time, were released twice a day into Quincy Bay with the outgoing tides. This treatment system was used into the 1970s, with engineers and scientists speculating that the harbor's currents would carry the sewage well away from the city, where it would be oxidized by the water or assimilated by sea animals. We all know how well that theory worked out.

Today, Moon Island is owned by the city of Boston and connected by a causeway to the Squantum section of Quincy. It is a place where new classes of recruits take their first steps to becoming Boston firefighters. The Boston Fire Department's academy on the north side of Moon Island trains new recruits during fourteen-week sessions, and current firefighters receive ongoing education at the training center, which includes concrete structures used to simulate fire scenes. In addition, the Boston Police Department uses the island for a shooting range and disposal of suspected bombs and other explosives. Due to these uses, access to Moon Island is understandably restricted.

Moon Island as seen from Thompson Island.

Diving into Boston Harbor

Thanks to ever-improving water quality in Boston Harbor, an increasing number of recreational divers are hunting for lobsters and exploring shipwrecks on the ocean floor. David Robinson, state underwater archaeologist for the Massachusetts Board of Underwater Archaeological Resources (BUAR), talks about what divers need to keep in mind while submerged.

"The Massachusetts Board of Underwater Archaeological Resources is the sole trustee of the Commonwealth's underwater heritage, promoting and protecting the public's interests in these resources. We encourage people to visit sites but not to disturb them. No one can damage, displace, or destroy an underwater resource without the board's permission. The exception is with exempt shipwrecks, which preserve such sites for the continued enjoyment of the recreational diving community.

"The outer harbor tends to attract more diving interest, but now that the harbor is clearing up, I think we'll see some activity coming back to the inner harbor. Most of the activity in the outer harbor is lobstering. There are a number of burned barges submerged in the general area of Calf Island that have a lot of structure, which the marine growth love and makes for very good lobstering."

Ships at Boston Harbor. *"In-going out-going" by Eric Lumsden is licensed under CC BY-ND 2.0.*

Exempted Shipwrecks

Currently, the BUAR lists three exempted sites in the Boston Harbor:

City of Salisbury: This steel freighter sank on April 22, 1938, bound for New York with a cargo valued at $2 million that included tropical animals. The *City of Salisbury*'s fate came at the long end of a troubled voyage: a Himalayan bear escaped while in Calcutta, a king cobra cannibalized its mate while at sea, and twenty-five monkeys jumped ship in Halifax. As Captain Lewis steered the ship toward the outer harbor a thick fog rolled in and the vessel impaled itself on uncharted rocks. Luckily, the pythons, cobras, monkeys, and rare birds were removed before the ship broke in two. Talk about invasive species!

Kiowa: The *Kiowa* was a steel freighter built in 1903 at Philadelphia and sank on December 26 of the same year. Due to blinding snow and poor visibility, Captain I.K. Chichester anchored the vessel near the approach of Nantasket Roads. The *Admiral Dewey*, another steamer bound for Jamaica, collided into the *Kiowa* as it was leaving Nantasket Roads. The force of the collision almost capsized the *Kiowa*, and the ship began to take on water fast. The *Cormorant*, an inbound tugboat, answered the *Kiowa*'s distress signals and Captain Chichester ordered his crew to jump for their lives. The U.S. government eventually removed the wreck as it was an impediment to navigation. Today, most of the remaining debris is flat.

Romance: This steel-hulled passenger vessel sank just north of Graves Light in Broad Sound on September 9, 1936. *Romance* and its 208 passengers were returning from a day trip to Cape Cod when another steamer, the *New York*, emerged from an impenetrable fog, a scant six hundred feet from the *Romance*'s port beam. Attempts to avoid a collision were unsuccessful, and it became clear that the *Romance* would go down. Within fifteen minutes of the collision the *Romance* was already assuming its watery resting place—luckily, everyone aboard had been evacuated. Located within the Boston shipping channel, the *Romance* is considered "deep, dark, and dangerous." Charters who frequent this wreck typically require advanced certification.

For more information, visit mass.gov/orgs/board-of-underwater-archaeological -resources.

A relief from the monument to Civil War dead at Long Island's cemetery.

Long Island

WHEN DENNIS LEHANE CONJURED UP the setting for his novel *Shutter Island*, which was made into a Hollywood thriller, he tapped into a childhood experience on Long Island when his uncle terrified him with creepy ghost tales about patients in the island's old hospital. While Shutter Island and its sprawling hospital for the criminally insane are fictitious, it mirrors the real-life history of the Boston Harbor Islands.

For centuries, Boston turned to its harbor islands to sequester and provide for those suffering from the physical and social ills that tend to fester in urban environments. For decades after social institutions disappeared from the rest of the harbor islands, the tradition of providing vital human-service programs endured on Long Island, where until 2014 the Boston Public Health Commission served close to one thousand people every day in a variety of programs that included homeless shelters, mental health treatment facilities, and drug and alcohol detox programs.

Those programs shuttered, however, when structural safety concerns forced the closing of the 3,200-foot bridge connecting Moon and Long Islands in 2014. The eventual demolition of the bridge superstructure (the support piers remained in the harbor) has further limited access to an island with as much history as any in Boston Harbor.

For decades, the campus on Long Island carried on the harbor's long tradition of assisting those in need. *Nicole L. Vecchiotti.*

For decades, the campus of buildings on Long Island hosted Boston social service programs.

The grotto of the shuttered chapel on Long Island.

Archaeological digs on Long Island have unearthed stone tools and pottery dating back nine thousand years. The island that sustained Native Americans for millennia became a dark place in 1675 and 1676 during King Philip's War when it was among the islands used by colonial authorities as internment sites. Hundreds, perhaps thousands, of Native Americans died on the islands from starvation and exposure. With such a long history, the possibility of unmarked human remains on Long Island is high, and tribes whose ancestors died on Long Island consider it a sacred burial ground.

In colonial times, due to the height of its three drumlins and its strategic location commanding the entrance to the inner harbor, Long Island played a key role in Boston's military history. During the Revolutionary War, Long Island provided a much-needed source of livestock and hay for the British holed up in Boston. On a July night in 1775, Continental Army soldiers snuck onto the island, stole the cattle and sheep, and took seventeen Loyalist prisoners. The patriots even launched a daring daylight raid the next morning to burn the remaining farm buildings and seventy tons of bundled hay that was about to be shipped to the British in Boston.

After the British fled Boston in March 1776, General George Washington's army occupied Long Island and built defensive batteries on its northern bluff. In June 1776, a fierce battle erupted as the troops fired on a British transport ship carrying Scottish reinforcements—apparently, the Scots hadn't been informed that their fellow soldiers had already skipped town. Approximately forty Scottish soldiers were killed, and it's possible they were buried somewhere on the island.

During the Civil War, soldiers traveling to and from the battlefields of the South drilled and trained at Long Island's Camp Wightman. The camp was later renamed Fort Strong in honor of Civil War general George Crockett Strong. During both world wars, enlisted men at the fort were responsible for laying and controlling mines in the northern channel of Boston Harbor. Even after the fort was deserted at the conclusion of World War II, Long Island housed two Nike missile batteries in the 1950s. (The city used one of the abandoned missile base buildings in the 1970s to store surplus books from the Boston Public Library.)

Hidden under a thick blanket of vegetation, crumbling bunkers and concrete gun emplacements from Fort Strong still occupy Long Island Head, the drumlin on the northeastern tip of the island. Near those ruins, barely peering above the ever-growing tree line, is Long Island Head Light. The current white brick lighthouse, dating from 1901, rises fifty-two feet in height and is the fourth beacon to grace the island's northern bluff.

At the base of Long Island Head is Camp Harbor View—a co-ed summer camp whose founding was spearheaded by advertising executive Jack Connors and late Boston mayor Thomas Menino—which hosts more than one thousand children from Boston neighborhoods at no cost. Activities include boating, arts, athletics, music, and aquatics. For many children, the camp—which includes a climbing wall, high ropes course, swimming pool, art pavilion, and a great hall named in Menino's honor—is their first introduction to the harbor.

This is not the first summer camp on Long Island, however. At the turn of the twentieth century, the Municipal Camp for Boys hosted as many as one thousand campers each summer for week-long programs focused on recreation and discipline. Unlike Camp Harbor View, boys wore uniforms, camped in tents, and rose to a reveille at six o'clock each morning. The present-day incarnation is a far kinder, gentler place, providing boys and girls ages eleven to fourteen arriving by ferry with the true summer experience every child deserves.

To the south of Camp Harbor View is the institutional campus that once hosted a city hospital and the Boston Public Health Commission programs. In the 1880s, after failed attempts to develop the island as a resort, the city of Boston purchased most of the island to host its charitable institutions. A hotel, built in the 1840s, was converted into an almshouse for the indigent and a chronic disease hospital; a nursing school and a home for

To FORT INDEPENDENCE
LONG ISLAND,
—AND—
FORT WARREN.

THE FAVORITE STEAMERS

ARGO & MAY QUEEN

Will leave FOSTER'S WHARF for Fort Independence, Long Island and Fort Warren, each making Four trips daily, as follows :—

To Fort Independence and Long Island at 9, 10, 12, 1, 2 1-4, 3, 5 and 7 o'clock.

To Fort Warren at 9 and 2 1-4, touching at Long Island and Fort Independence both ways.

The 9, 1, 3 and 5 trips by the MAY QUEEN.   The 10, 12, 2¼, and 7 by the ARGO.

The Last Trip, (7 o'clock,) will be made to Fort Independence and Long Island ONLY; the boat remaining at the latter place over night, and leaving for Boston at 8 o'clock the next morning, touching at Fort Independence.

FARE down and back, 50 Cents.

Passengers by these boats can stop at Fort Independence, Long Island or Fort Warren on either trip, and resume their journey at pleasure, with the same ticket, (which is good for the day,) on either of these boats.

A MOONLIGHT EXCURSION!

Will be made by the Steamer ARGO, **ON TUESDAY EVENING, July 23d,** at 8 o'clock. TICKETS 50 CTS. A Band of Music will be in attendance.

J. E. Farwell & Co., Steam Job Printers, No. 32 Congress St., Boston.

unwed mothers were added later. To make room for these new residents, the city forcibly removed a small village of Portuguese fishermen living on the east side of the island in 1887. Many of the Portuguese fishermen floated their shacks across the harbor and settled on Peddocks Island, creating the cottage colony that still endures.

Weather, time, and neglect have taken their toll on some of the brick buildings huddled in the middle of Long Island that include a former FBI safe house, chapel, morgue, and a boarded-up theater that once hosted Hollywood legends who entertained the troops at Fort Strong. On the south side of the island, a stark white cross ravaged by the elements towers over a cemetery that could hold as many as 3,500 of the sick, outcast, and unwanted who passed away in island institutions. An adjacent Civil War monument contains the names of seventy-nine Union veterans flanking a haunting angelic image who were buried nearby.

Although Long Island has a number of historical sights and great potential as a recreation area, public access is restricted because of the safety hazard from aging structures.

The beacon of Long Island Light peeks up from the tree line on the north side of the island.

Boston Light Swim

Above: Elaine K. Howley at the finish line of the 2007 Boston Light Swim. *Elaine K. Howley.*

Left: Rose Pitonof in her swimming leotard, 1910. *Courtesy of the Library of Congress.*

One August day in 1910, little Rose Pitonof swam through Boston Harbor, head bobbing up and down in the surf with every breaststroke. Rose was on her way to the record books and international fame by becoming the first woman—and only the second person—to swim the nearly ten-mile distance from the pier of Charlestown Bridge to Boston Light on Little Brewster Island. (Alois Anderle had been the first person to complete the swim, but his result was disputed because he crawled over the bar at Nixes Mate during low tide.) Battling cold water, crosscurrents, winds, and waves, Rose completed the swim in six hours and fifty minutes. Seven men tried to make the journey that day. All gave up. What made Rose's amazing feat all the more remarkable was that she was only fifteen years old.

Banner headlines on the front page of *The Boston Globe* trumpeted the accomplishment of the "stocky little phenomenon of the water." News of Rose's accomplishment quickly spread around the world. Suddenly propelled into fame, Rose spent the next six years headlining a renowned vaudeville circuit, performing diving and swimming feats in a water tank before sell-out audiences across the country. She continued to set long-distance swimming records in Boston, New York City, and London.

Today, long-distance swimmers such as Elaine K. Howley carry on the proud tradition of traversing the harbor in the annual Boston Light Swim. Held every August, the eight-mile swim from Boston Light to the L Street Bathhouse in

South Boston is called the "granddaddy of American open-water swims." The race draws elite open-water swimmers from countries as far away as Egypt.

There's nothing "light" about the effort required to complete the Boston Light Swim. Conditions can be grueling. These marathon swimmers battle powerful crosscurrents, boat traffic, and strong gusts of wind. But it's the frigid water, even in August, that can pose the greatest challenge. "As soon as you jump into the harbor, you feel the air rush out of your lungs," says Howley.

The course record is under two and a half hours, but depending on conditions, most swimmers finish in between three and five hours, which is the time limit for competitors to reach the city. For swimmers like Howley, the achievement is awe-inspiring. "Approaching the city skyline from the water is powerful; here I am swimming toward one of the world's most important cities, seeing it from an angle that few other people experience."

Those who prefer to stay dry can participate in the Boston Light Swim by serving on support boats that offer food, drink, and lots of encouragement to the swimmers. But whether you're manning the boat or bobbing along, there's no question about it—you're immersing yourself in history.

For more information, visit massowsa.org/bls.

ADDITIONAL INFORMATION

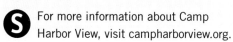
For more information about Camp Harbor View, visit campharborview.org.

A boardwalk to a marsh on the
east side of Thompson Island.

Thompson Island

DESPITE THE FACT THAT IT IS ONLY a twenty-five-minute boat ride away, Thompson Island exudes the feeling of the deep wilderness. The rustling of birds and animals can be as startling as the wind blowing through the trees, and hours can pass without seeing another person—though abandoned campsites may have you wondering if you truly are alone. This eerie sensation is heightened when the path in front of you suddenly opens onto a clearing filled with startling structures reminiscent of military training grounds. Towering, wooden formations fastened together like teepee frames soar above the tree line, and a colossal web of rope looks as if Spider-Man himself had recently visited. Just when you're ready to panic, the Boston skyline comes into view along with the comforting reminder that civilization is within easy reach of this rustic sanctuary.

Henry Adams sardonically wrote of his hometown that "Boston is a curious place. Its business in life is to breed and to educate." Well, for nearly two hundred years Thompson Island has been fulfilling that latter civic obligation. Today, the Thompson Island Outward Bound Education Center proudly continues the tradition of using the island in educational service.

Farm School students fresh from the fields. *Courtesy Archives and Special Collections Department, Healey Library University of Massachusetts Boston. Thompson Island Collection.*

Signs direct visitors on Thompson Island.

Long before its ultimate purpose was divined, however, Thompson Island was a hunting, clamming, and fishing ground for Native Americans. An exploratory band of ten Pilgrims, in a quest to contact and trade with the Massachusett tribe, was among the first Europeans to set foot on the island's shores in 1621. Led by Miles Standish and with Squanto as a guide, it took almost a full day for the Pilgrims to reach Boston Harbor from Plymouth in their tiny shallop; but when they finally arrived, they were awed by the island-dotted harbor. "Better harbours for shipping cannot be than here are," they reported. So impressed were the Pilgrims that they regretted the hand of God had not guided them to Boston Harbor as their final destination in the New World. William Bradford, governor of Plymouth Colony, wrote that the expedition "brought home a good quantity of beaver, and made report of the place, wishing they had been there settled (but it seems the Lord, who assigns to all men the bounds of their habitations, had appointed it for another use)."

Standish and the Pilgrims claimed the island for a Scot, David Thompson, who was the acting governor of New England and said to be the first

European settler in New Hampshire. In 1626, Thompson established a trading post on the island to swap beaver furs and fish with the Native Americans. His cabin on the eastern side of the island may have been the first permanent colonial structure in Boston.

The island was granted to Dorchester in 1634, and the town voted in 1639 to rent it to property holders for twenty pounds a year. The income afforded the town a schoolmaster, who taught writing, English, Latin, and other languages to mainland children, beginning the island's long-running connection with educating the city's youth.

It wasn't until nearly two centuries later, however, that Thompson Island's educational mission was formally realized. A group of Boston philanthropists, concerned about the welfare of boys in the city, purchased the island and established the Boston Farm School to teach them agricultural and vocational skills. It is believed that Charles Bulfinch—the famed architect who designed the Massachusetts State House—drew the plans for the great brick Greek Revival building perched on the island's summit that housed most of the school's students and faculty. The inaugural class of fourteen boys arrived on Thompson Island in 1833, and an educational institution of one sort or another has remained there ever since.

The Farm School band. *Courtesy Archives and Special Collections Department, Healey Library, University of Massachusetts Boston. Thompson Island Collection.*

City Hall on Cottage Row. *Courtesy Archives and Special Collections Department, Healey Library, University of Massachusetts Boston. Thompson Island Collection.*

Soon after it opened, the Farm School merged with the Boston Asylum for Indigent Boys, which was founded in the wake of the War of 1812 to care for boys left orphaned and destitute by the fighting. Students divided their time between farm work, study, and play. They also performed domestic duties such as cooking, baking, and laundry. Students planted oak, maple, and many other trees along with pear and apple orchards, many of which remain today. These Farm School vestiges make Thompson Island one of the few places on the harbor islands where mature woodlands are found.

The school was granted legal guardianship of the boys until they reached the age of twenty-one. Even though many students were in clear sight of home, they could only return to visit during two weeks in the summer. Author Nathaniel Hawthorne, who visited the island in 1837, noted how detached the boys were from the constant activity of Boston and its busy harbor. "The farm boys remain insulated," he wrote, "looking at the passing show, within sight of the city, yet having nothing to do with it; beholding their fellow-creatures skimming by them in winged machines, and steamboats snorting and puffing through the waves. Methinks an island would be the most desirable of all landed property, for it seems like a little world by itself."

One of the Farm School's claims to fame is that it was home to the first school band in the United States. In 1857, Headmaster William Morse overheard a group of students entertaining themselves with a makeshift "orchestra," outfitted with instruments made from combs covered by tissue paper. Seizing upon their initiative, Morse bought his students brass instruments, and the band was formed. Six school alumni would go on to become members of the Boston Symphony Orchestra.

The school also provided a unique model community, dubbed Cottage Row—and if Hawthorne thought the school was a little world unto itself in 1837, he should have seen Cottage Row more than fifty years later. Cottage Row began in the summer of 1888 when some of the boys erected a row of

The ruins of the root cellar once used by the Farm School on Thompson Island.

tents on the north end of the island in which they lived. The next year, using skills they'd learned from their manual training, the boys erected twelve wooden cottages. Possession of these small, one-room cottages dotting the shoreline was divided into shares transferable through the school bank.

Cottage Row became a mock city that served as a practical civics lesson for the boys. The cabins included a city hall and a library of three hundred volumes. The boys elected a mayor, assessor, clerk, police, street commissioner, and jury members. An appointed judge oversaw judicial proceedings, and justice could be severe. A group of boys arrested for playing marbles on Sunday faced fines of up to thirty-five cents; another boy convicted of annoying the goat was condemned to feed and water "Nannie" for a month.

In the 1900s, the school became known as the Farm and Trade School. Students from ten to fourteen years of age split their time between studying and learning an industrial trade or occupation, such as carpentry, cabinetry, woodworking, mechanical drawing, blacksmithing, and printing. The school's print shop even provided Boston hotels with their handbills, and three upper grades had practical study in meteorology.

Over the years, a variety of interesting—and strange—proposals have been floated for Thompson Island. For example, in the 1990s the city of Boston proposed using the island as a training camp for the New England

Thompson Island is one of the closest islands to downtown Boston.

Patriots football team. But the most grandiose plan called for the island to be part of a site for a huge international exposition in 1976 to celebrate the American bicentennial. The planners of Expo '76 projected that up to sixty million people would visit the 690-acre fairground, which, in addition to Thompson Island, would have been located on Columbia Point in Dorchester and a new harbor island created from a combination of landfill and floating platforms.

The plan called for construction of a five-hundred-boat marina and a hotel on the southern end of Thompson Island as well as the conversion of the school facilities into a youth camp and demonstration farm. Visitors would have been able to rent bikes or electric cars to traverse the island. The exposition planners' strangest idea, however, was to build a huge, transparent dome that would cover part of the island's natural landscape of grassy knolls, woods, and winding trails. This climate-controlled dome, more than two football fields in diameter, would ensure that boating, swimming, and picnicking could be enjoyed year-round—even in the throes of a New England winter. These elaborate plans never came to fruition, and the island remains true to its educational legacy.

Since 1988, the island has been privately owned by the Thompson Island Outward Bound Education Center. Although the organization works with youth from all economic backgrounds and adults as well, its primary mission is to serve underprivileged Boston children by offering programs that instill teamwork, compassion, and self-confidence through experiential learning. Thompson Island Outward Bound serves more than five thousand students and adults each year. Students camp, scale those towering climbing walls, traverse that wily ropes course, and engage in mock search-and-rescue activities on and off the island. The island is a living outdoor laboratory for students to explore nature and learn about biodiversity. Corporations and youth group programs also use the Outward Bound facilities on Thompson Island for team-building retreats.

Given the vast amount of programming offered, Thompson Island is only open to public exploration on weekends from Memorial Day until Labor Day, but clearing a Saturday or Sunday to make the trip is worth it. As one of the largest and most ecologically diverse islands in the harbor, it's easy to spend an entire afternoon hiking through its 204 acres of meadows, salt marshes, freshwater ponds, woodlands, and dunes.

Ferries leave from the EDIC dock at the Marine Industrial Park in South Boston, delivering you to the island in twenty-five minutes. Nearest the dock on Thompson Island are administrative buildings along with private classrooms, a library, a dining hall, an auditorium, and a gymnasium. The quad of brick dormitories on the top of the hill will remind you of a leafy, Ivy League campus. There is also a conference center that hosts business meetings, catered events, and even weddings.

Away from the campus, a network of mowed pathways and dirt trails crisscross the island's deep woods and rolling meadows. Along with a northerly trail along the beach is a 1.5-mile loop from the dock to the southern side of Thompson Island that includes waymarked signs and Farm School remnants such as the shell of the root cellar that once kept four thousand bushels of fruit and vegetables dry behind two-foot-thick masonry walls. One of the highlights on the southern loop is the forty-acre salt marsh. The largest marsh on the Boston Harbor Islands, with its rivulets and tall grasses, serves as a nursery for fish and shellfish and is a popular stop-over in the spring and fall for migrating shorebirds such as yellowlegs, geese, sandpipers, and teals. In the summer, herons, egrets, and killdeers can be found nesting in trees, and in the winter, buffleheads and mergansers take up residence in the marsh.

The southern end of Thompson Island contains one of the most poignant plots of land on the Boston Harbor Islands, a cemetery containing the unmarked graves of Farm School students and island residents, including boys who drowned in two of the most tragic events in the harbor's long history. In April 1842, as a reward for good behavior, a large group of students was treated to a fishing trip on the harbor. In sight of the Thompson Island shore and some of the other boys who attended the school, the *Polka*, the school's sloop, suddenly overturned and sank. Twenty-three boys, a teacher, and a boatman all drowned. Only four boys survived. *The Boston Evening Transcript* reported of the incident: "It is one of those events of an inscrutable Providence, which occurring suddenly to so many youthful spirits, in the moment of joyous exhilaration and sending sorrow and mourning into so

Colorful flowers on Thompson Island.

many families, cannot but excite in the breast of everyone a sympathy for the bereaved families, and a lively sense of the frail tenure of human existence."

Fifty years later, tragedy unfortunately struck again as another school sloop capsized between Spectacle Island and Thompson Island in a sudden squall. Ten students and an instructor were thrown into the frigid harbor and clung to the overturned craft, praying for a rescue that never came. The chill of the water and exhaustion were too much as they fell one by one into the sea. Four hours after it overturned, the boat drifted ashore with just two survivors still clutching the hull.

The graveyard includes Native American remains discovered at a burial site on the northern end of the island and reinterred here. Only a few jagged pieces of broken headstones remain. Most markers had been removed due to vandalism, and it is believed they were subsequently lost in a 1971 fire that destroyed the original Farm School building.

Arthur Pearson, Outward Bound

The Thompson Island Outward Bound Educational Center provides "adventurous and challenging experiential learning programs that inspire character development, compassion, community service, environmental responsibility, and academic achievement." Arthur Pearson, president of the nonprofit organization, explains how the island location helps it to fulfill its mission.

"The physical attribute of having an island is that it—and any island—has its own charisma and allure by the nature of being separate and apart. Each one has its own character and personality. And by providing a vest pocket wilderness, Thompson Island allows us to do very powerful outdoor programming very close to home. For many kids in metropolitan Boston, it's their first time in the harbor or on a boat of that size, and stepping on the island's shore, they are as far from home as they have ever been, at least mentally and spiritually. Just that physical attribute of being a refuge is very powerful. We have the best of both worlds. We are right in the heart of the city with the ability to really feel and be in a wilderness environment.

"Some of the most magical places with students young and old are the climbing towers and ropes course. In some ways, it's the great equalizer. It's as important for the corporate chieftain as it is a fourteen-year-old starting something new and a lot of remarkable growth happens out there for children of all ages. The places many of our students also find to have a powerful impact on them, though in a much quieter way, are the salt marshes and shorelines where one can really capture a sense of the tranquility that Mother Nature offers when you are able to stop and listen."

The challenge course used by Outward Bound participants on Thompson Island.

Near the cemetery on the island's southern tip is a massive sand spit, exposed at low tide, that reaches to Squantum on the mainland in Quincy. The mudflats in this area were a popular clamming spot for centuries. On the western side, a curved beach provides views across Dorchester Bay to the John F. Kennedy Library and the National Grid gas tank, that colorful landmark familiar to everyone who's sat in traffic on the Southeast Expressway. The beach becomes sandier on the eastern shore of the island, facing Spectacle Island.

A small salt marsh on the easterly shore, which had been previously drained to grow hay to feed farm animals, has been restored to allow tidal flow to resume. With the reestablishment of tidal flushing, native salt marsh

Grassy paths lead visitors along Thompson Island.

grasses have returned to this side of Thompson Island along with migrating shorebirds, which can be watched from a viewing platform at the end of a wooden boardwalk.

The marsh also provides a nursery for schools of fish, which will feel right at home on Boston's island classroom. And this small piece of wilderness in Boston's backyard continues to deliver lessons. By calling to the adventurer in each of us, Thompson Island teaches us about ourselves, our community, and our environment.

An information board greets visitors at the end of Thompson Island's dock.

ADDITIONAL INFORMATION

 Thompson Island is only open to public exploration on Saturdays and Sundays from Memorial Day to Labor Day. Pack bug spray along with food and drinks as there are no concessions available on the ferry or on the island.

 The *MV Outward Bound* ferry dock at EDIC Pier is located off Terminal Street near the Raymond L. Flynn Black Falcon Cruise Terminal and the Boston Design Center in South Boston's Marine Industrial Park. The island encourages visitors to arrive early. There is a nearby public parking lot at 12 Drydock Avenue, and the nearest Silver Line station is Harbor Street. At the time of publication, roundtrip ferry fare is $17 for adults, $10 for children ages three to twelve, and free for children under age three. For more information and ferry schedules, visit thompsonisland.org.

 Three moorings located off of Thompson Island are available for free on a first-come, first-served basis. Note that there is no public access to Thompson Island from these moorings. Private boaters are not permitted to land on the island.

Around Hingham Bay

Peddocks Island

THE BOSTON HARBOR ISLANDS ARE FILLED with ruins of forts, hospitals, and other buildings that remind us of their rich collective history, and these shadowy remnants give us great insights into the city's unique heritage. But for centuries, the islands have also been called "home" by those who lived on their shores, providing countless personal, intimate memories of island life that the skeletons of old buildings simply can't begin to share.

Today, the collection of approximately twenty summer cottages on Peddocks Island is the only community that remains on the Boston Harbor Islands. It's the last breathing connection to generations past, and these stalwart islanders endow Peddocks Island with a unique and wonderful character.

While some cottages have fallen into disrepair, others are quaint, well-kept clapboard homes adorned with lobster traps and buoys, painted in a bright rainbow of colors. The history of the island is as colorful as the cottage paint jobs. The antecedents of some cottages date to 1887, when Portuguese fishermen and lobstermen floated (yes, floated) their families and houses over the open harbor to Peddocks Island after being forced to move from Long Island. There are captivating stories of bootleggers and gamblers in addition to childhood memories of carefree summer days that have spanned as many as five or six generations back to the original Portuguese lobstermen. This living history may not have much life left in it, however. Under an agreement with the state, the current islanders are slated to be the last of those allowed to live on Peddocks Island.

Islanders like to say Peddocks Island, located just a quarter mile from the Nantasket Peninsula across Hull Gut, is actually five islands in one because of its composition of five drumlins connected by sandy, gravel bars called "tombolos." The double drumlins of East Head contain the ruins of Fort Andrews; Middle Head is home to the summer cottages; while West Head and Princes Head offer

The canopy of foliage overhead on the
West Head of Peddocks Island.

A marsh on Peddocks Island.

nearly pristine environments. Since 210-acre Peddocks Island is one of the harbor's largest and has the longest shoreline, it's easy to spend hours wandering the rocky beaches and exploring its varying topography, perhaps the most diverse of all the harbor islands. The trails on Peddocks Island take you past woodlands, scrubby sandbars, rocky beaches, brackish ponds, and salt marshes.

The island gained its name after English planter Leonard Peddock in the early 1600s, though there is evidence that Peddocks Island has been inhabited for thousands of years. One day in 1971, summer resident Josephine Walsh was digging for soil for her cottage's rose bushes in the side of an eroded bluff on West Head when she was shocked to discover a skeleton. Carbon dating determined the bones to be 4,100 years old, making it the oldest skeleton ever found in New England at the time.

Europeans started farming the island as early as 1634, and the agricultural uses of Peddocks continued well into the following century. Peddocks, not unlike other harbor islands, was one more site on which the day-to-day struggles of the Revolutionary War played out. Both the patriots and British often turned to the island farms to seize supplies for their armies, or simply

Built in 1941, the chapel on Peddocks Island is one of the last of its design still standing.

strip their foes of much-needed provisions. Indeed, in 1775, just a few months into the Revolutionary War, patriots raided a Loyalist farm on Peddocks Island and seized four hundred sheep and thirty head of cattle. The following year, six hundred patriot militiamen were stationed on the island to discourage the evacuated British from returning to the city.

Peddocks Island's destiny as a military site didn't end there. With the construction of Fort Andrews in 1898 at the onset of the Spanish-American War, the island played a role in protecting the city of Boston. The fort was built on eighty-eight acres donated by Eliza Andrews, widow of a former Massachusetts governor, and named in honor of her uncle, Civil War general Leonard Andrews. Opened in 1904, Fort Andrews housed artillery, gun batteries, and observation stations and was used heavily during World War I, preparing soldiers before their deployment to Europe. It was decommissioned after the war but reactivated with the onset of World War II.

One of the most noteworthy episodes in Fort Andrews' history may also be its most charming. During the latter half of World War II, more than one thousand Italian prisoners of war captured in North Africa were detained in the fort. The prisoners were originally held on Deer Island and in Camp

McKay in South Boston, but after the fall of Italian dictator Benito Mussolini and the surrender of Italy in 1943, the prisoners—no longer considered a threat—were moved to Fort Andrews and given considerable liberties. Peddocks Island was certainly no German stalag. In fact, American veterans were known to complain about the "pampering" of the former enemy forces. During the week, the Italian POWs worked at the Charlestown Navy Yard loading munitions on American ships bound for the European theater of war. When they weren't working, the Italian soldiers were relatively free to move about the island and played soccer on the fort's parade ground. They were given passes to visit Boston in groups of ten to twenty-five, provided they were chaperoned by a U.S. Army sergeant, and they could even receive visitors on weekends.

Italian American families living on Peddocks Island and around Boston befriended many of the prisoners, some of whom lived in the same towns in Italy from which the American families had emigrated. It wasn't uncommon to see the prisoners in the North End on Sundays. The prisoners spent the day going to Mass and eating a home-cooked meal with sponsor families before taking the ferry back to the island. Italian American women brought the prisoners food and supplies, and in some cases they fell in love and married. There were approximately fifty marriages between POWs and daughters or relatives of sponsor families.

At the conclusion of World War II, the Italians who hadn't married Bostonians were sent back to their homeland, and the fort was abandoned. The East Head of the island, once completely barren, is now abundant with trees. Park management spent $15 million to make the fort ruins safe for visitors by stabilizing and abating fourteen dilapidated brick buildings and demolishing a dozen that were beyond repair.

At the foot of the pier stands the fort's former guardhouse, which has been renovated and converted into a ranger-staffed visitor center that has bathrooms and island information. Visitors can wander among the fort's crumbling, concrete mortar batteries and surviving buildings—which include the former barracks, bakery, gymnasium, fire station, and storehouse—although they are now boarded up for safety reasons. Four brick homes on Officers Row survive, but the rest were torn down. That land has now been converted to a group campground with picnic tables and charcoal grills.

If you'd like to sleep under the stars on the Boston Harbor Islands but are more of a "glamper" than a camper, Peddocks Island is the place for

Visitors walk by the Welcome Center at the end of the dock on Peddocks Island.

you. Nestled among the trees atop East Head is a campground with six yurts that feature screen doors, skylights, bunk beds, tables, and benches. The

wood-and-canvas structures also sport electric outlets that you can use to keep your phone charged. You'll want it to take photos of the sunrise over Boston Light from a magnificent scenic overlook just steps away from the campground.

Next to the dock and parade ground is a small, white chapel built in 1941 that served the fort and island residents of all denominations. From a distance, the wooden chapel looks as if it was transplanted from the rolling hills of Vermont. The provenance of the chapel, which included a choir loft

A yurt offers creature comforts to campers on Peddocks Island.

The dock at Peddocks Island.

...ful Adirondack chairs with the Peddocks Island chapel in the background.

and government-issued pipe organ, is quite interesting, however. It was one of hundreds built according to a military template used during World War II and believed to be among the last of its design still standing. A 2014 refurbishment breathed new life into the chapel, and there are hopes to eventually make it available for weddings and other events.

The rusty fence that separated Fort Andrews from the civilian side of the island still stands, and a small stone marker imprinted with "US" is implanted in the beach on the island's west side. Within the boundaries of the fort on East Head, the asphalt roads remain. Once outside the fort, however, they become unpaved trails, with a single path leading from the dock all the way to the other end of the island at West Head. After leaving East Head, the trail traverses a tombolo flanked by rocky beaches and placid coves. Reaching Middle Head, the topography changes again; the trees return and the land rises once more.

Near the spot where the trail ascends Middle Head is the former site of the Island Inn, which was a popular destination for summer outings and boating parties in the early 1900s. The hotel was owned and operated by John Irwin, a former professional baseball player in the 1880s and 1890s. In the first decade of the twentieth century, Irwin helped organize "Ye Olde-Timers' Gambol," an annual reunion of retired ballplayers from as far back as the 1860s that drew upward of two thousand players and fans. (One of the big stars was Arthur Cummings, considered the inventor of the curve ball.) The highlight of the day was a baseball game with the retired players in what may have been the first old-timers' game ever organized in the United States.

Drunken parties, brawls, gambling, and prostitution all helped the Island Inn to earn its notorious reputation as the "Headache House Hotel." In 1909, following a "Chinese picnic," a euphemistic term for an opium party, Hull police arrested Irwin on charges of maintenance of a nuisance, illegal gaming, and illegally selling intoxicating liquors. William Drake, proprietor of the nearby West Head House and a former policeman, was also arrested and similarly charged. The complaints were filed by representatives of the Watch and Ward Society, whose censorship of books and performing arts was the origin of the phrase "Banned in Boston." Both men were found guilty and had to pay a small fine.

Drake's hotel burned down in 1913, and Irwin's hotel was gone a few years later. A small blue cottage on the eastern shore, which was at one time adjacent to the main lodge, is all that remains from the wild days of the Island Inn. The cottage's charming exterior belied some of the nefarious activities that took place inside. Revelers could drink the night away at the bar on one side of the cottage, while ladies of the night plied their trade in bedrooms on the other side.

It may not be quite as lively, but the cottage colony on Middle Head has a vibrant history as well. When the government purchased the land on East Head for the construction of Fort Andrews, the Portuguese fishermen and lobstermen who had relocated there from Long Island once again floated their shacks, this time to Middle Head. During Prohibition, the community had a flourishing bootlegging business, and rumrunners were known to hide their cargo in the island's coves. (And soldiers in search of a lobster dinner and some hooch were known to visit the island's civilian side.)

Summer residents joined the Portuguese lobstermen on Peddocks Island, drawn by its pure air, cool nights, and lulling waves. At its peak, the cottage village had hundreds of residents during the summer months. A general store sold goods to residents, and the Tea Room sold penny candy and ice cream. Middle Head even had its own unofficial "mayor," Mabel Pinto.

Today, the scene on Middle Head is quite different. There are far fewer residents, occupying a hodgepodge of quaint cottages and ramshackle shacks. (There are a handful of year-round residents on Peddocks Island,

The Living History of Peddocks Island

Claire and Bill Hale are among the last cottagers on Peddocks Island. Their two-story cottage on the former site of John Irwin's Island Inn has been in Claire's family since 1948, and she shares her memories of summers on the island.

"My family has been coming here since 1917. My uncle did business with the Portuguese fishermen. When my uncle told them his son had rickets, they told him to come to Peddocks Island and put him out in the sun for the summer. So he rented a cottage and stayed all summer. And when he took the boy back to the doctor in the fall, his legs had straightened out. So my uncle bought a cottage.

"When my father came to this country from Italy, he was eleven years old. Peddocks Island was the first place his older brother took him. And when my father met my mother, he took her here and she fell in love. My father came here until he was seventy-five years old. At one point our family had ten cottages on Peddocks. We turned the island from Portuguese to half-Italian!

"During the war, the Italian prisoners started coming to the cottages on Sunday when they didn't have to work. They had a grand old time. I remember all these soldiers with 'Italy' written on their uniforms. Just before they were sent back, my grandmother had them visit our house in Somerville. Our house was surrounded by MPs with guns. We were the only Italians on the street in a mostly Irish neighborhood, so you can imagine all the neighbors were on their porches.

"When I was a teenager, we would go to Princes Head every single night and have a bonfire. We sang 'Goodnight Irene' at the end of the bonfire. Without the cottages, Peddocks is going to lose history that started with the Portuguese fishermen from the Azores who came here to help the fishing industry in Boston. It will be a shame."

One of the colorful cottages on Peddocks Island.

An outhouse to one of the cottages on Peddocks Island.

too.) There is no electricity or running water in the cottages since the power and water lines were severed. Residents rely on gasoline-powered generators, propane, oil lanterns, car batteries, and solar panels for power and light. Rainwater is collected in plastic rain barrels, and some cottages have well water.

Even more difficult for longtime islanders is the sense that they've become *persona non grata* in the eyes of the state, which took ownership of Peddocks Island in 1970. The state has sought to evict the islanders, arguing that the cottages are private use of public land and a source of pollution. A compromise reached in 1992 allows the present residents to remain until their deaths. At that point, the cottages will pass into the ownership of the state. Currently, cottagers pay an annual permit fee to the state, which owns the land but not the structures. Since the compromise was reached, residents have passed away or given up their homes, and the number of cottagers continues to dwindle as the years pass by.

The West Head of Peddocks Island offers a sharp contrast to the summer colony of Middle Head, as it is largely uninhabited. At a pink cottage on Middle Head, the main path across the island veers to the left and traverses another sandy tombolo. Once on West Head, this grassy pathway leads through dense foliage, enveloping you in a breathtaking tunnel of green. The path ends at a narrow, rocky beach with a view directly across the water to Nut Island. During World War II, for fear of German U-boats wandering into the Boston Harbor, submarine nets were erected between the West Head and Nut Island (and across Hull Gut from Fort Andrews to Hull, too).

The elevated, eroding bluff of Princes Head juts off from the east side of Peddocks Island, and is where soldiers at Fort Andrews practiced military maneuvers. In the 1870s, the bluff was the target for cannon tests taking place at Nut Island (see page 216). To walk out to Princes Head, approach it from the north, along the beach near Middle Head.

Despite being barren as recently as sixty years ago, Peddocks Island has evolved into a vibrant ecosystem. The ruins of Fort Andrews are surrounded by a dense woodland of mature and sapling pine, maple, birch,

A cove on the shore of Peddocks Island.

Waysigns on Middle Head of Peddocks Island.

and cottonwood trees, which attract owls and hawks. Apple and pear trees from the U.S. Army orchard remain. Succulent blueberries and blackberries abound in August, and cherries and Concord grapes are also common. The brackish pond on West Head is one of only two black-crowned night heron rookeries in the state. Deer, turkeys, and coyotes frequent the island, and wandering off pathways is not recommended because of the prevalence of ticks.

In 2018, Boston Harbor Now in partnership with the National Park Service and Massachusetts Department of Conservation and Recreation began to undertake a long-term project to redevelop and attract more visitors to Peddocks Island. Ideas being considered included everything from a luxury hotel and spa to an artist retreat to a green-energy research center. What the future holds is unknown, but what is certain is that if the cottages disappear, the last connection to living history on the Boston Harbor Islands will be extinguished. Hopefully a solution can be found that will permit the roots of those who call Peddocks Island "home" to endure, while allowing new generations to create their own personal memories of this fascinating island.

Princes Head on Peddocks Island.

ADDITIONAL INFORMATION

 Group and individual campsites are available on Peddocks Island. Reservations are required and can be made online at ReserveAmerica .com or by calling toll-free (877) 422-6762. At the time of publication, reservations for tent sites cost $8 for Massachusetts residents and $10 for non-residents and are available daily from late June to early September. In addition, six electrified yurts that can sleep six people are also available. Yurt campers must bring linen or sleeping bags. At the time of publication, reservations for yurt sites cost $55 for Massachusetts residents and $70 for non-residents and are available daily from late June to early September. Campgrounds have composting toilets, drinking water, picnic tables, and charcoal grills but there is no on-island food concession. Campgrounds are in high demand, so make reservations early. Reservations are taken as much as six months in advance. For campground availability, call (617) 223-8666.

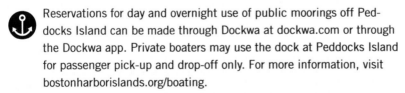 Reservations for day and overnight use of public moorings off Peddocks Island can be made through Dockwa at dockwa.com or through the Dockwa app. Private boaters may use the dock at Peddocks Island for passenger pick-up and drop-off only. For more information, visit bostonharborislands.org/boating.

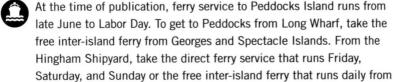 At the time of publication, ferry service to Peddocks Island runs from late June to Labor Day. To get to Peddocks from Long Wharf, take the free inter-island ferry from Georges and Spectacle Islands. From the Hingham Shipyard, take the direct ferry service that runs Friday, Saturday, and Sunday or the free inter-island ferry that runs daily from Georges Island. For ferry schedule, visit bostonharborislands.org.

The dock at Bumpkin Island contains an outdoor exhibit area. The stone building to the right served as a pump house for the naval training station.

Bumpkin Island

PART OF THE CHARM AND EXCITEMENT of exploring the Boston Harbor Islands is that you never know what you will stumble upon. This is certainly the case with Bumpkin Island, where a grassy path through the woods leads to the remnants of an old stone farmhouse dating back to the early 1800s. Its round stones and arched doorways make it look as though it was plucked from the Irish countryside. The roof is gone, and its insides are overgrown with trees, but the outer shell has withstood the passing of about two hundred years, during which Bumpkin Island was transformed from farmland to home for a children's hospital to the site of a World War I naval training center.

Long before that, however, Native Americans traveled to Bumpkin Island during the summer months to dig for clams, hunt waterfowl, and gather fruits, nuts, and berries. Following the arrival of European settlers, the island was granted to Weymouth in 1636. At the time it was called Round Island. Like the rocks used to build the farmhouse, Bumpkin has an oval shape with a single sandbar snaking back toward Hull's Nantasket Peninsula that can be crossed at low tide.

In the mid-1600s, Samuel Ward obtained the island by royal grant. Upon his death, Ward bequeathed the island to Harvard College, thus providing the Boston Harbor Islands with a touch of the Ivy League. Ward gave the island to Harvard with the provision that it never be sold, although rental income could go to the college "for the easement of the charges of the diet of the students that are in [the] Commons." He also stipulated that the isle be known as Ward's Island. No such luck. Bumpkin stuck—maybe because it's just more fun to say than Ward's. (At times, the island has also been known as Bumkin, Bomkin, and Pumpkin.)

Throughout the next two centuries, Harvard leased Bumpkin Island for $50 a year to tenant farmers. At the turn of the twentieth century, Albert Cameron Burrage—a wealthy lawyer, copper magnate, and civic leader—arranged to lease Bumpkin Island from Harvard for five hundred years.

The charming stone farmhouse on Bumpkin Island dates back to the early nineteenth century.

The Burrage mansion on Commonwealth Avenue, circa 1903. *Courtesy of the Library of Congress.*

Something of a renaissance man, Burrage remains an interesting figure in the city's history, and by the end of the nineteenth century he was highly regarded in Boston society. As a political and civic activist, he served on the Boston Commerce Council and was the brains behind the Burrage Ordinance of 1892, which prohibited city employees from becoming involved in political action groups. Burrage was also appointed to the Boston Transit Commission, charged with the task of creating Boston's first subway system. A passion for horticulture (Burrage was renowned for the tropical orchids he cultivated) even led him to serve as president of the Massachusetts Horticultural Society for a period of time.

Burrage's tremendous success in business allowed him to live grandly, as shown by his chateau-style mansion at 314 Commonwealth Avenue. With its elaborate exterior stonework that includes dragons and gargoyles, the Burrage mansion remains an architectural highlight on any Back Bay tour today. Burrage's interest in Bumpkin, however, was solely in the name of philanthropy.

The Burrage Hospital, which opened in 1902, provided care and treatment for poor children with physical disabilities. Burrage had been awakened to the need for such a facility following a football injury that left his son confined to the house for weeks on end. While the hospital accepted children suffering from almost any non-contagious disease, crippled children received particular attention. According to *The Boston Globe*, the island was an ideal place for the hospital because "its location is such that the cooling winds that always prevail here and the bright sunlight are depended upon to a great extent for cures."

The hospital dominated the crest of Bumpkin Island's drumlin, providing a commanding outlook from its perch seventy feet above the water. Charles Brigham, the architect who designed the old Museum of Fine Arts in Copley Square and Burrage's mansion, built the hospital with yellow brick, terra

Bumpkin Island War Song

The November 3, 1918, edition of the *Boston Sunday Advertiser* included sheet music for new and popular songs to support the American cause in World War I. The featured song in the newspaper was "Bumkin Island" by the Boston Naval Reserves. Here are the lyrics that accompanied the music written by Mrs. G.L. Camden:

We sing of an isle that's a gem of the deep
Where sailors are made by the score
Where none but the hardiest sailor can keep a footing on its rock-bound shore
But we love it all the same and we love its dear old name
Though we work all the day rain or fair
So we'll learn to fight on the top of its height
Till we're called to the front over there

Bumkin Island! Bumkin Island!
The fairest spot in the sea
With the luster of the diamond
A spot where I love to be
Bumkin Island! Bumkin Island!
May your fame be spread a far
You're a jewel dropped from sky-land
For you'll help us win the war

We come from ev'ry walk and phase of life
All eager to respond to the call
With hardly any knowledge of military strife
And without much experience at all
But we're changing now from dubs to the men who'll down the subs
And we'll surely be a credit to your name
For we'll make the Hun take all hurdles on the run
And the Kaiser will be wiser at the game

Bumkin Island! Bumkin Island!
The fairest spot in the sea
With the luster of the diamond
A spot where I love to be
Bumkin Island! Bumkin Island!
May your fame be spread afar
You're a jewel dropped from sky-land
For you'll help us win the war

cotta, Indiana limestone trimmings, and a green slate roof. It was constructed in the shape of the letter H and equipped with wheelchair ramps to accommodate its patients. The children were able to enjoy the harbor views from a ten-foot-wide veranda running along its front.

The hospital could house as many as 150 children at a time. A daily steamer traveled between Boston and Bumpkin Island, and a doctor at the dock received patients and made arrangements for their stay. Parents were permitted to visit on Saturday, but only children could remain on the island.

Bumpkin Island was such an idyllic summer location that The Randidge Fund, another charitable endeavor in the early 1900s, sponsored daily island trips for poor children in Boston. Children spent the day on the island frolicking in the water, playing baseball, and enjoying picnics. In some years, the fund supported outings for as many as fifteen thousand children in a summer season.

As the United States prepared to enter World War I, Burrage closed the hospital and transferred his island lease to the federal government for the grand sum of $1 a year. (To assist the war efforts, Burrage also lent the government his 260-foot steam yacht, the *Aztec*. Dismayed by the yacht's condition when it was returned to him after the war, Burrage filed a claim against the federal government and is said to have successfully recouped $300,000 of the $385,000 he'd requested for repairs.)

The U.S. Navy took over Bumpkin Island as a training station, adding fifty-six temporary and wooden structures to the island by the end of 1917. The hospital building was transformed into naval headquarters and a sickbay. Toward the end of the war, German prisoners of war who had been held on Gallops Island (see page 42) were transferred to Bumpkin Island.

The naval station garrisoned upward of 1,750 men at a time—a number on par with Fort Warren, Fort Andrews, and the other military instillations on the Boston Harbor Islands—and graduated nearly 15,000 seamen before the war was over. In addition to their training, the enlisted men endeavored in other pursuits. In fact, music proved to be an important part of life for the reserves stationed on Bumpkin Island, with a twenty-three-piece band giving regular concerts on the veranda of the former hospital building. The sailors also played organized games of baseball and football. In 1917, a squad from Bumpkin Island squared off on the gridiron against Harvard University (the island's rightful owner) in Harvard Stadium. While the sailors lost 35–0, it's worth noting that Harvard was a pigskin power in the 1910s, eventually capturing four national championships during the decade.

When the war was over, almost all of the naval buildings were torn down or dismantled and rebuilt on shore. The cracked asphalt roads crossing the island are some of the few reminders of Bumpkin's days as a naval training station. On the north side of the island, near the shell of the old stone farmhouse, are the ruins of the station's mess hall. At its height, the mess hall fed all the Bumpkin Island troops in thirty minutes flat. Chunks of concrete have crumbled to the ground, poison ivy and other plants climb the remaining walls, the terrazzo floor is no more, and the roof is missing—but close your eyes and you can hear the music, the clinking silverware, and the lively mealtime chatter masking the certain dread trainees must have felt about their pending trips to the front.

The Navy left Bumpkin Island after the war, and Burrage's hospital reopened only for a brief time in the summer of 1940 to treat children with polio. In 1946, the hospital was destroyed by a spectacular blaze, visible for more than ten miles around. Today, the hospital site looks as if a river of red and yellow bricks swept in to flood an open pit. Within this sea of bricks only small sections of the hospital's edifice remain intact. The spruce trees, which once guided patients and visitors to the hospital's grand entrance,

A mess hall facade is one of the last remaining vestiges of the naval training station that once stood on Bumpkin Island.

now serve to conceal what remains of the structure. (Watch out for poison ivy if you decide to explore the ruins.)

Like many of the harbor islands, centuries of agricultural use left Bumpkin Island bleak and treeless. (In fact, Frederick Law Olmsted had proposed a reforestation plan for the Boston Harbor Islands, including Bumpkin, in the 1890s. See page 208.) Today, the scene is much different. Invasive species and trees planted around the hospital grounds have filled in the landscape, and Bumpkin Island is brimming with blackberries, bayberries, dewberries, raspberries, and elderberries. Summer sees pink and white sea roses and yellow wildflowers, set against staghorn sumac, gray birch, and quaking aspen. Pear and apple trees can also be found along the thirty-acre island's paths.

Roads once part of a naval training station are now walking trails on Bumpkin Island.

Bumpkin Island has long been a popular place for picnickers, and the picnic area, situated in a wide expanse on the state-owned island's southwest corner, provides a picturesque view of Hingham Bay and Slate and Grape Islands. Campgrounds are available off the long straight path that bisects the island.

It is on the north side of Bumpkin Island that you will be treated to its most spectacular vista. There, the Boston skyline is perfectly framed by the Middle and East Head of Peddocks Island. Rising from the tombolo connecting those heads, the soaring edifices that form the backbone of the city reach for the sky. It's a great place to enjoy the restorative summer breezes that attracted Burrage and so many others through the years to Bumpkin Island.

ADDITIONAL INFORMATION

 Group and individual campsites are available on Bumpkin Island. Reservations are required and can be made online at ReserveAmerica .com or by calling toll-free (877) 422-6762. At the time of publication, reservations cost $8 for Massachusetts residents and $10 for non-residents and are available Friday and Saturday nights from late June to early September. Campgrounds have composting toilets, picnic tables, and nearby charcoal grills but there is no on-island running water, electricity, or concessions. Campgrounds are in high demand, so make reservations early. Reservations are taken as much as six months in advance. For campground availability, call (617) 223-8666.

 For boaters arriving by private craft, docks are for passenger pick-up and drop-off only.

 At the time of publication, ferries to Bumpkin Island run Friday, Saturday, and Sunday from late June to Labor Day. To get to Bumpkin Island from Long Wharf, take the free inter-island ferry from Georges Island. Ferry service also runs from the Hingham Shipyard to Bumpkin Island.

Seagrass along the shoreline of Grape Island.

Grape Island

A FEW STEPS FROM THE DOCK on Grape Island, a set of inviting Adirondack chairs beckon from under the shady canopy of a soaring evergreen. It is a fitting welcome to this picturesque, secluded island. Unlike many of the Boston Harbor Islands, the fifty upland acres that make up Grape Island have been spared the scars left by the large-scale construction of forts, hospitals, and social institutions. It is this nearly pristine environment that makes Grape Island the most rustic camping island in the harbor and an unparalleled draw for nature lovers. Grape Island is *the* place to get away from it all, reconnect with the great outdoors, and feel as if you are in the woods of northern New England, rather than eight miles from downtown Boston.

With a name like Grape Island, you might expect to see a landscape teeming with tangled vines. While the state-owned island is said to have received its name from the wild grapes that once attracted European settlers, there are none on the island today. (Though, a grape arbor near the dock is a nod to the island's name,

Deer frequent Grape Island.

not to mention the perfect place to wait for the ferry on a hot day.) What you will find, however, is an island filled with a wide variety of interesting flora and fauna that you could spend hours exploring.

Native Americans were drawn to Grape Island for thousands of years. In the 1800s, tomahawks were commonly discovered on the island, and in the 1970s archaeologists unearthed a midden—a large waste deposit of shells and refuse left behind by indigenous peoples. Lack of development on Grape Island over the years means there is the potential for other archaeological finds in the future.

After the Europeans arrived, they used the island primarily for farming and grazing, with the last permanent residents of Grape Island leaving in the 1940s. A foundation of a nineteenth-century farmhouse near the dock is one of the few remaining signs of the island's agricultural past. The farmhouse also served as the island caretaker's cottage during the first half of the twentieth century, when the island was owned by the Bradley Fertilizer Company, which had a large operation across the channel on Weymouth Neck. The fertilizer company used the island to graze horses and harvest hay for the Bradley family polo grounds in Hingham. Those polo grounds eventually became the Hingham Shipyard, which contributed over 227 ships, largely Destroyer Escorts, to the war efforts during World War II. The rich history of the Hingham Shipyard remains a significant source of pride for South Shore residents today.

The agricultural use of Grape Island triggered the island's most notable historic event—a colorful armed skirmish during the Revolutionary War. While every school-age child is familiar with the battles at Lexington and Concord that launched the American fight for independence, very few realize that the next armed confrontation between the British and Boston colonists wasn't at Bunker Hill. It was at Grape Island.

Following the devastating battles at Lexington and Concord, the beleaguered British troops and their sympathizers found themselves under siege and holed up on the peninsula of Boston in desperate need of supplies. With land routes cut off, the British set their sights on the farms of the Boston Harbor Islands, which remained readily available to them as their naval supremacy remained intact.

On the morning of May 21, 1775—a little more than a month after the battles at Lexington and Concord and a little less than a month before the battle at Bunker Hill—the Grape Island Alarm began. That morning, a small British force set out in four boats for the island with the hopes of seizing cattle, vegetables, and hay for horses and livestock. At the time, Grape Island was owned by Elisha Leavitt, a Loyalist living in Hingham. Old Elisha offered up his farm's provisions to the British army, thereby becoming, in the eyes of his patriot neighbors, a turncoat for the redcoats.

British boats sailing toward the south shore of Boston Harbor presented a troubling sight to the colonists, and wild rumors quickly spread that as many as three hundred redcoats were launching an attack on Hingham, Weymouth, or another neighboring town. General alarms began to sound. Bells pealed and guns fired to rouse the militia. When the patriots finally arrived at Weymouth Neck, they discovered the British weren't attempting a land invasion as feared but loading their boats with hay from Leavitt's farm across the channel.

The good news for the revolutionaries was that the British force was much smaller than originally reported. The bad news was that the militia had arrived at low tide and was therefore forced to wait until the flats were covered by the flood tide in order to launch their boats. The colonists anxiously watched for hours as the British made the long trip from barn to boat and back again, carting Leavitt's hay as they went. To make matters more vexing, the distance across the water was too great for the militia's small arms to be of any use. They fired in vain anyway, with the British vessels returning fire as their troops worked. Finally, the tide was high enough for the colonists to attack—but no sooner had the Americans launched their boats than the British returned to their ships and set sail for Boston with the few tons of hay they had successfully removed. The colonists, exchanging fire with the retreating redcoats, landed on Grape Island and proceeded to burn Leavitt's barn to the ground, along with its remaining seventy to eighty tons of hay. Leavitt's cattle were spared but relocated to the mainland.

An angry mob of patriots set out for Leavitt's house in Hingham to exact retribution, but catching wind of their coming, Elisha was ready. Not with a rifle, it is said, but with cheese and crackers, cake, and a barrel of rum. The refreshments did the trick and calmed the patriots. After all, who wouldn't trade a little hay for some spirits and light fare?

The bucolic atmosphere on Grape Island today provides no hint to the confused events that took place on that day more than two hundred years ago. After the last resident left and the agricultural use of the island ceased, Grape Island developed into a woody, shrubby landscape. Grassy paths loop around the circumference and down the middle of the island. At certain spots, the trails are walled in by bushes measuring more than five feet high. Numerous benches provide wonderful harbor views, although some vistas are becoming obscured by growing foliage.

A grove of staghorn sumac on the shoreline of Grape Island.

The Letters of John and Abigail Adams

Abigail Adams was one of the colonists roused by the Grape Island Alarm. John Adams, who would become the country's second president, was away from the couple's saltbox house in present-day Quincy to attend the Second Continental Congress in Philadelphia. Their letters to each other provide a window into some of the early confusion and fear about the intent of the British forces.

Letter from Abigail Adams; Braintree, Massachusetts
May 24, 1775

"I suppose you have had a formidable account of the alarm we had last Sunday morning. When I rose, about six o'clock, I was told that the drums had been some time beating, and that three alarm guns were fired, that Weymouth bell had been ringing, and Mr. Weld's was then ringing.

"I immediately sent off an express to know the occasion, and found the whole town in confusion. Three sloops and one cutter had come out and dropped anchor just below Great Hill. It was difficult to tell their designs; some supposed they were coming to Germantown [in Braintree], others to Weymouth; people, women, children from the iron works came flocking down this way— every woman and child above or from below my father's. My father's family flying, the Drs. [Dr. Cotton Tufts'] in great distress, as you may well imagine for my aunt had her bed thrown into a cart, into which she got herself, and ordered the boy to drive her off to Bridgewater, which he did.

"The report was to them that three hundred had landed, and were upon their march into town. The alarm flew like lightning, and men from all parts came flocking down, until two thousand were collected. But it seems their expedition was to Grape Island for Leavitt's hay. There it was impossible to reach them, for want of boats; but the sight of so many persons, and the firing at them, prevented their getting more than three tons of hay, though they had carted much more down to the water.

"At last they mustered a lighter, and a sloop from Hingham, which had six port-holes. Our men eagerly jumped on board, and put off for the island. As soon as they perceived it, they decamped. Our people landed upon the island, and in an instant set fire to the hay, which, with the barn, was soon consumed, about eighty tons, it is said. We expect soon to be in continual alarms, until something decisive takes place."

Letter from John Adams; Philadelphia, Pennsylvania
June 10, 1775

"I long to know, how you fare, and whether you are often discomposed with alarms. Guard yourself against them, my dear. I think you are in no danger—don't let the groundless fears, and fruitful imaginations of others affect you. Let me know what guards are kept—and who were principally concerned in the battle at Grape Island, as well as that at Chelsea. The reputation of our countrymen for valor is very high. I hope they will maintain it, as well as that for prudence, caution, and conduct."

Letter from Abigail Adams; Braintree, Massachusetts
June 22, 1775

"You inquire of me who were at the engagement at Grape Island. I may say with truth, all Weymouth, Braintree, Hingham, who were able to bear arms, and hundreds from other towns within twenty, thirty, and forty miles of Weymouth . . . Both your brothers were there; your younger brother [Elihu], with his company, who gained honor by their good order that day. He was one of the first to venture aboard a schooner to land upon the island."

Like many of the Boston Harbor Islands, Grape Island is filled with staghorn sumac, so named because their hairy upper stems and flower stalks resemble a deer's velvety antlers. Staghorn sumac, whose fuzzy red berries can be harvested to brew a cold drink called sumac-ade, is considered a pioneer species on the harbor islands as it is among the first plants to return to an area that was disturbed by activities such as fire, agriculture, and deforestation. Groves of other early successional species such as gray birch and quaking aspen also cover the island.

Although a visit to Grape Island would be delightful any time of year, the island explodes with color from its profusion of wild berries during the summer—including six edible varieties, among them raspberries, blueberries, and blackberries. Thanks to these berry bushes, Grape Island is a haven for wildlife. The berries attract a wide variety of birds, such as songbirds, quail, and pheasant. Wintertime brings snowy owls and bald eagles. The stags appear to be as plentiful as the staghorn sumac, and with so many deer on the island, be on guard for ticks. Visitors to the island may also encounter wild turkeys, raccoons, and—hold your nose—skunks.

Wild turkeys can be found on Grape Island.

Grape Island lies just five hundred yards offshore from Weymouth Neck and is composed of two drumlins connected by a marshy lowland. The island's west drumlin is the larger of the two, rising seventy feet above sea level. Three shaded benches on this side of the island provide an expansive view of the harbor and the city from the John F. Kennedy Library in Dorchester all the way to the Bunker Hill Monument in Charlestown.

On the north side of Grape Island, paths lead to a stony beach that has the look and feel of a secluded cove; the long, curved shoreline will have you wondering why you didn't bring your beach chair and umbrella. The rocky beach on the east side of the island is filled with the colorful shells of blue mussels, white soft-shell clams, and periwinkles. Huge Roxbury puddingstone boulders are strewn along the western shoreline.

The south side of the island is home to a marshy lowland that contains plants such as salt-spray roses, salt-water cordgrass, and seaside goldenrod. Some of the slate bedrock that underlies Boston Harbor is visible as an outcrop on this side of the island. Marsh wildflowers, such as jimson weed, beach pea, and scarlet pimpernel, can be found near the beach.

Grape Island's natural surroundings make it a favorite camping experience for many on the Boston Harbor Islands. Its wooded campsites are away from the visitor paths, providing some privacy. While other islands such as Bumpkin, Peddocks, and Lovells have noteworthy remnants of human development, camping on Grape Island will really make you feel like you're roughing it. And there's one added benefit of camping on Grape Island. Those Adirondack chairs are even more inviting come sunset.

Campers disembark on Grape Island.

A campground sign on Grape Island.

Adirondack chairs offer a welcoming seat near the Grape Island dock.

ADDITIONAL INFORMATION

 Group and individual campsites are available on Grape Island. Reservations are required and can be made online at ReserveAmerica .com or by calling toll-free (877) 422-6762. At the time of publication, reservations cost $8 for Massachusetts residents and $10 for non-residents and are available Friday and Saturday nights from late June to early September. Campgrounds have composting toilets, picnic tables, and nearby charcoal grills but there is no on-island running water, electricity, or concessions. Campgrounds are in high demand, so make reservations early. Reservations are taken as much as six months in advance. For campground availability, call (617) 223-8666.

 For boaters arriving by private craft, docks are for passenger pick-up and drop-off only.

 At the time of publication, ferries to Grape Island run Friday, Saturday, and Sunday from late June to Labor Day. To get to Grape Island from Long Wharf, take the free inter-island ferry from Georges Island. Ferry service also runs from the Hingham Shipyard to Grape Island.

Grape Island sports the most rustic of campgrounds on the Boston Harbor Islands.

Hangman Island

THE HAUNTING NAME OF DESOLATE Hangman Island is apropos. Hangman Island is composed of rugged granite and slate rocks, which Bostonians quarried in colonial times. Coupled with the eroding power of the sea, the removal of the island's stone reduced Hangman Island to less than an acre in size at high tide. Only three feet above sea level, its low elevation can make the island difficult to spot when the tide is high.

Located in Quincy Bay due west of Peddocks Island, the exact origin of Hangman Island's appellation is unknown. According to one legend, pirates were executed and hung up in gibbets on the island, though there are no historical records to prove it. Another story has it that a hermit living on the island also served as the county hangman.

What is known is that Hangman Island was a seasonal home in the late 1800s and early 1900s to a handful of fishermen and lobstermen who lived in modest, wooden shacks; and they were known to courageously answer the distress calls of mariners in the harbor surrounding the island.

The only residents of state-owned Hangman Island these days are gulls, ducks, and other seabirds. A small, pebbly beach on the southern side offers a landing spot, but Hangman Island is difficult to approach because of the many rocks and hidden shoals in the immediate area.

These chickens are a curious throwback to the island's colonial days as a pasture for grazing sheep. *Sherman "Pat" Morss, Jr.*

Sheep Island

IT'S HARD TO IMAGINE LOOKING AT IT TODAY, but Sheep Island was a sizable plot of land in colonial times. The island was once twenty-five acres in size and large enough to be used for grazing sheep, hence its name. But centuries of pounding wind and water have reduced Sheep Island to a sliver of land between Grape and Peddocks Islands, measuring just a few acres.

During the late 1800s and early 1900s, the island was used for recreational outings, including an annual trip by members of the Sheep Island Club, which included prominent Boston politicians and businessmen. Each year, the club sailed to Sheep Island, set up a tent, and enjoyed an afternoon feast of chowder. Apparently, this was quite an affair. It took about five hours to cook the chowder, eat the chowder, "talk the chowder over," and go home. Decades later, Sheep Island proved a less hospitable place for pleasure seekers. A hermit reportedly lived on the island, and it was said he'd shoot anyone daring to land on its shores.

Covered by scrubby vegetation, sumacs, and marsh grass, the state-owned island is accessed by beach landing, but there is little to see. It is a nesting site for birds, and visitation is discouraged during nesting season because birds can be aggressive—although perhaps not as combative as a gun-toting hermit.

Slate Island, from Grape Island. *Nicole L. Vecchiotti.*

Slate Island

EVEN THOUGH IT LIES JUST 250 YARDS EAST of Grape Island, Slate Island is geologically different from its neighbor. Grape Island is composed of two glacial drumlins, while Slate Island consists of slate outcrops.

As early as the 1600s, the island's slate was used in the construction of houses in and around Puritan Boston. Nathaniel Bradstreet Shurtleff, an author and mayor of Boston between 1868 and 1870, wrote in *A Topographical and Historical Description of Boston* that "although the material has not been of a remarkable quality for the protection of roofs, it has done good service for underpinning and for cellar walls." The blue-colored slate was also used to make some of the gravestones that can be seen in Hingham Cemetery today, and remnants of the quarrying activity can still be found on the island. In the 1930s, the Davis Bates Clapp Memorial Association, a charitable nonprofit organization, ran a short-lived summer camp for boys on Slate Island.

A rocky beach on the island's southwestern shore is a good landing spot for kayaks and flat-bottomed boats, but the lack of trails, dense underbrush, and poison ivy make it difficult to explore the state-owned island's twelve-acre interior.

Sherman "Pat" Morss Jr.

Raccoon Island

TINY RACCOON ISLAND, LITTLE MORE THAN three acres in size, lies just two hundred yards off the shore of Quincy's Houghs Neck peninsula. This state-owned bedrock outcropping in Hingham Bay is so close to shore that it is accessible across the mudflats at low tide. Any visitors to Raccoon Island, which was used for grazing sheep during colonial times and housed a summer retreat for the Stigmatine Fathers in the 1930s, should be mindful of the bounteous poison ivy growing in the island's interior.

Many colorful characters have lived on the Boston Harbor Islands over the years, but Clifford H. Jenks, who bought Raccoon Island in 1923, was undoubtedly one of the more eccentric. According to *The Boston Globe*, Jenks was known as "the Human Fly," an appellation he earned by scaling the sides of buildings.

Shortly after buying Raccoon Island, Jenks tried to perform another daring feat—he wanted to bring his car to the island from the mainland. Unfortunately, the car got stuck in the mudflats. Ever resourceful, Jenks tied empty barrels to the car and managed to float it the rest of the way at high tide. Of course, the more interesting story might be *why* Jenks needed a car on the tiny island in the first place.

Sarah Island, Langlee Island, and the Boston skyline in the distance. *Nicole L. Vecchiotti.*

Hingham Harbor Islands

ON SUMMER WEEKENDS, HINGHAM HARBOR is awash with seagoing vessels of all shapes and sizes. Kayakers paddle across the blue sheet of water, sailors hoist billowing sails, and yacht owners carry on the town's proud nautical tradition while listening to the Red Sox game on the radio.

Hingham has always been a seafaring town, built on the backs of the fishing and shipbuilding industries. During Hingham's maritime heyday in the nineteenth century, it was common to gaze upon wooden mackerel fishing fleets heading out to sea or yachts racing in fevered competition. Magnificent steamers, some of them capable of carrying as many as 1,500 people, plied the harbor on their routes between Hingham, Boston, and Nantasket.

While the types of sea craft have changed over the centuries, one constant in Hingham Harbor has been its four picturesque islands—Button, Langlee, Sarah, and Ragged. And these small,

The Hingham Yacht Club. *Nicole L. Vecchiotti.*

rocky islands, owned by the town of Hingham, are pleasant spots to explore. All four islands are in close proximity and can easily be visited in a morning or afternoon, and they are particularly popular with kayakers, who can launch from the town beach on Hingham Harbor. Boaters can reserve moorings amid the Hingham Harbor Islands and along the shores of World's End from the town's harbormaster.

According to local folklore, Hingham resident John Langley named the three northernmost islands in the harbor (Sarah, Ragged, and Langlee) after his beautiful, but raggedly dressed daughter Sarah. While Langley did own these islands in the late 1600s, the legend that he lived on the islands as a poor fisherman is apparently untrue. In reality, Langley was an innkeeper and a boatyard owner, although Sarah and her friends probably spent summer days playing on the islands. John Langley's daughter grew up to be Sarah Langley Derby, who in 1784 endowed one of the oldest coeducational private schools in the United States—Hingham's venerable Derby Academy.

Although you would never know it today, another Hingham institution once occupied the harbor's western shore. For a quarter of a century, Hingham's Crow Point neighborhood was home to Melville Garden, one of New England's finest resorts in the late nineteenth century. Wealthy Boston industrialist Samuel Downer, who built his fortune in the kerosene business, spent a quarter of a million dollars to turn his private estate, located along present-day Downer Avenue, into an enchanting pleasure ground that he named after his mother-in-law, who was a cousin of *Moby-Dick* author Herman Melville. Although a teetotaler himself, Downer modeled his amusement park after the German beer gardens that so captivated him on his European travels.

As many as seventy thousand people visited Melville Garden each summer between 1871 and 1896. Eleven times a day, steamboats departed from Boston's Rowes Wharf with visitors eager to leave the hot, crowded city to enjoy the refreshing sea breezes and amusements at Melville Garden. Park patrons could take a leisurely stroll around the beautiful grounds and its fine Victorian buildings. If they wanted a little more activity, they could take a swim, fish, shoot billiards, row around the harbor, play croquet, and listen to bands play in the music hall. For fifty cents, visitors could stuff themselves at the Rhode Island clam bake pavilion, which could seat more than one thousand diners at a time. Children were thrilled by the garden's "flying horses," Punch-and-Judy shows, and monkey cages. There was even a bear den.

After sunset, park patrons were amazed by the wonder of Melville Garden's twenty electric lights, the first in Hingham. And fireworks lit up the night sky every Tuesday and Thursday. At the end of the night, visitors could either take a steamer back to Boston or spend the night at the ornate eighty-room Rose Standish House.

Another popular attraction for visitors to Melville Garden was a ride on a side-wheel, hand-propelled boat to nearby Ragged Island, the westernmost isle in Hingham Harbor. The views from the island's gazebos, pavilions, and lookouts made it a popular picnicking spot for parasol-toting women and men nattily attired in their suits and bowler hats.

Sarah Island is a popular nesting spot for gulls, egrets, cormorants, and herons. *Nicole L. Vecchiotti.*

Today, Ragged Island is no longer a place to visit dressed in your Sunday best. Much of Ragged Island's four-acre interior is impenetrable due to overgrown brambles, and steep rock ledges surrounding the island make it difficult to circumnavigate. There is a small rocky cove on the island's northeast side on which to come ashore. Watch out for poison ivy and the thickets that will have you thinking "jagged" would have been a more appropriate name for the island.

East of Ragged Island, Sarah Island offers a better opportunity for exploration. A gravelly beach on the north side of the island offers the best location to come ashore, as thirty-foot-high ledges flank the island's southern shore. Adjacent to the beach are mudflats filled with salt grass and large tidal pools that resemble water-filled craters. While there are no trails, Sarah Island is more passable than Ragged, though there is considerable undergrowth on the western side of the island.

Sarah Island, once known as Sailor's Island before its purchase by John Langley, is a popular nesting spot for gulls, egrets, cormorants, and herons. In the springtime, the birds' chorus rises from the rookeries and fills the air

Ragged Island sits in Hingham Harbor.

Treasures from the tide pools.
Nicole L. Vecchiotti.

around the island. Keep in mind that visitation to four-acre Sarah Island is greatly discouraged during nesting season, as birds tend to be very territorial.

John R. Brewer, the owner of World's End, purchased Sarah and Langlee Islands in 1860 for the sum of $250. At that time, the islands, like World's End, were barren landmasses. In the early 1890s, Brewer planted trees at World's End according to plans drawn up by Frederick Law Olmsted (see page 208); he extended the reforestation to his two islands. Numerous maples, oaks, elms, and cedars that were planted by Brewer's employees remain on Sarah Island today.

On eight-acre Langlee Island, the leafy canopy of these now-mature oaks, maples, and cedars offer welcome shade. A picnic table below a grand old oak tree in the middle of the island is particularly inviting. There are no paths on Langlee Island, but thanks to its mature woodlands, it is the easiest of the Hingham Harbor islands to explore. A five-person campground on the west side of the island and a ten-person campground on the east side of the island can be reserved through the town's harbormaster.

Langlee Island sits in Hingham Harbor.

A small beach on the northwest side of Langlee Island offers a place to come ashore. Above the beach is a forty-foot-high cliff of Roxbury puddingstone that provides the best vantage point in Hingham Harbor. This outlook offers views of the harbor from nearby Crow Point to downtown Boston in the distance. Make sure to check out the view beneath your feet, too. Roxbury puddingstone is a conglomerate composed of rocks of all different shapes, sizes, and colors cemented together by geological forces. The end result is something that looks a little like Christmas pudding. Unless you're a geologist, you probably didn't know that Roxbury puddingstone is the state rock of Massachusetts. (But be honest—did you even know there *is* a state rock?)

Low tide is an interesting time to explore Langlee Island's tidal mudflats—filled with hermit crabs, barnacles, and eelgrass—on its western side. The southeast shore of Langlee Island includes a sweeping sandbar and sandy beach, which offers another spot to come ashore.

Button Island, the southernmost island in Hingham Harbor, received its name because of its diminutive size of less than an acre. There are no trails on Button Island and not much to see besides a handful of trees and dense undergrowth of brambles. Getting ashore can be a challenge since the island is bounded by small rock outcrops, boulders, sand, and mudflats.

Thousands of revelers are drawn to the shores of Hingham Harbor around the Fourth of July to watch the fireworks launched from Button Island. The patriotic pyrotechnics hark back to the shows that lit up the night sky above the harbor and Melville Garden more than a century ago. The flying horses, wondrous Victorian buildings, and bear den may be long gone, but the Hingham Harbor islands are still there for our recreation and entertainment.

Climate Change and the Boston Harbor Islands

The black-and-white beacon standing upon the shoals of Nixes Mate serves as a warning not just for mariners transiting Boston Harbor but for anyone concerned about the future of the national park area. Thanks to Bostonians removing stone and slate from the shores of Nixes Mate for nearly two centuries, the former twelve-acre island melted into the harbor so that by 1805 all that remained were rocky flats submerged at high tide.

The destruction of Nixes Mate reminds us that the Boston Harbor Islands are under constant threat from man-made and natural forces and their future existence is far from guaranteed. The all-volunteer Friends of the Boston Harbor Islands selected the Nixes Mate day marker as its symbol because the island's fate demonstrates that stewards are required to ensure the preservation and conservation of the national park area so that it can be enjoyed by future generations.

In the twenty-first century, the Boston Harbor Islands face no bigger threat to their existence than rising sea levels caused by climate change. Emissions of greenhouse gases such as carbon dioxide and methane trap heat in the atmosphere, which results in warming ocean waters that produce more powerful storms, melt polar ice sheets, and take up more space than colder

Storms have caused the erosion of bluffs on Lovells Island.

Nixes Mate with the Boston skyline in the background.

waters. The sea level in Boston Harbor has risen by nearly a foot since 1921, according to the National Oceanic and Atmospheric Administration. That has made the city more prone to flooding. According to a climate study released by the city of Boston in 2016, the sea level of Boston Harbor may be as much as 1.5 feet higher in 2050 than it was in 2000 and as much as three feet higher in 2070.

Michael Creasey, general superintendent of the National Parks of Boston, says the harbor islands are already experiencing the impact of climate change and rising tides. "You can see the erosion on many of the islands right now, such as the north end of Peddocks Island and pretty dramatically on Georges Island right next to the fort wall. Much of the seawall has bucked up, and wind erosion has occurred."

On Gallops Island, powerful storms have worn away a shoreline cemetery and exposed bodies and coffins. "The erosion is destroying sites at an alarming rate," says Massachusetts Department of Conservation and Recreation archaeologist Ellen Berkland.

The Boston Harbor Islands protect the city by acting as natural barriers to temper the brunt of increasingly powerful Atlantic storms. Park management has been working with the Woods Hole Group to develop a regional flood model, and their analysis of wave energy has demonstrated the vital role played by the harbor islands in safeguarding downtown Boston.

"Based on actual storms that have occurred, they have found that seventeen-to twenty-foot waves off the Brewsters were reduced to two to three feet by the time they hit sections of Boston," says Boston Harbor Now president and CEO Kathy Abbott. "So if you remove the islands, the waves will obviously be much higher. That means there's a critical need to preserve the islands to provide that protection to the city."

To defend Boston from rising sea levels, some have proposed building upon nature's work by constructing enormous storm barriers across the harbor and among the islands, which could significantly impact their ecosystems. The University of Massachusetts Boston's Sustainable Solutions Lab esti-mated that a 3.8-mile gated harbor barrier from Winthrop to Hull that would incorporate Lovells, Gallops, and Georges Islands into its design could cost between $8 billion and $11.8 billion and wouldn't be functional until 2050 at the earliest. The researchers advised against the flood barrier because of its exorbitant cost and instead recommended that planners focus on shore-based coastal protection systems.

The National Park Service is partnering with Boston Harbor Now, the James M. and Cathleen D. Stone Foundation, and the University of Massachusetts Boston to study resiliency measures.

"Clearly the islands will be impacted more and more as sea levels rise. One thing we are looking at is how the islands can serve as models for protecting the mainland," Creasey says. "Planning is so important right now because change is occurring as we speak."

ADDITIONAL INFORMATION

 Secure moorings are available through the Hingham Harbormaster. Reservations and annual permit required. Call (781) 741-1450. For more information, visit hpd.org/198/Harbormaster.

 Free permits are required to camp on Langlee Island. Permit applica-tions are available from the Hingham Harbormaster website: hpd.org/198/Harbormaster. For more information, call (781) 741-1450. At the time of publication, a transient mooring for campers is available for $35 for a twenty-four-hour period. Note there are no restrooms on the island.

The Outer Harbor

Little Brewster Island

AS THE FERRY DOCKS AT LITTLE BREWSTER ISLAND, it is met by Sally Snowman, keeper of Boston Light, clad in an eighteenth-century costume. Her hand-sewn colonial dress and white bonnet recall the romantic days of lighthouses. Snowman's warm reception is appropriate for an island and lighthouse that has welcomed storm-tossed mariners from distant shores for more than three hundred years.

Little Brewster Island, the smallest of the Brewsters, is a rocky three-acre island. What it lacks in size, however, it makes up for in stature. This humble island is dominated by the distinguished, bold pillar of Boston Light, a postcard-perfect New England lighthouse. As the first light station built in the United States, Boston Light is not only the most historic structure on the Boston Harbor Islands, but also a revered National Historic Landmark.

In colonial days, the primary entrance to the harbor ran between Little Brewster Island and Point Allerton on the northern reach of Hull. Navigating the entrance could be tricky, particularly for captains unfamiliar with the harbor's layout. Before Boston Light, crude

The tower of Boston Light dominates
Little Brewster Island.

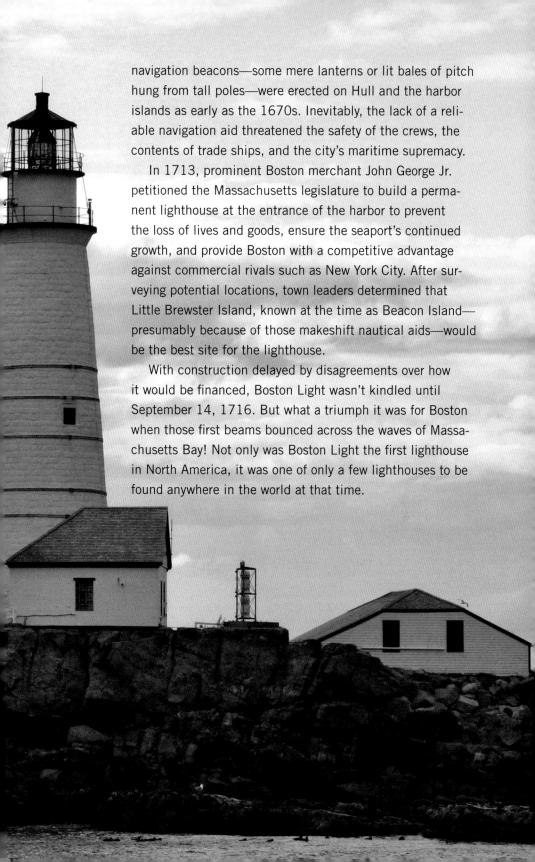

navigation beacons—some mere lanterns or lit bales of pitch hung from tall poles—were erected on Hull and the harbor islands as early as the 1670s. Inevitably, the lack of a reliable navigation aid threatened the safety of the crews, the contents of trade ships, and the city's maritime supremacy.

In 1713, prominent Boston merchant John George Jr. petitioned the Massachusetts legislature to build a permanent lighthouse at the entrance of the harbor to prevent the loss of lives and goods, ensure the seaport's continued growth, and provide Boston with a competitive advantage against commercial rivals such as New York City. After surveying potential locations, town leaders determined that Little Brewster Island, known at the time as Beacon Island—presumably because of those makeshift nautical aids—would be the best site for the lighthouse.

With construction delayed by disagreements over how it would be financed, Boston Light wasn't kindled until September 14, 1716. But what a triumph it was for Boston when those first beams bounced across the waves of Massachusetts Bay! Not only was Boston Light the first lighthouse in North America, it was one of only a few lighthouses to be found anywhere in the world at that time.

The lightkeeper's house on Little Brewster Island dates back to 1884.

A tax of a penny a ton on all vessels entering and leaving the harbor financed Boston Light's construction. The lighthouse tower was approximately sixty feet high and made of stone, although there was considerable woodwork around the structure and lantern frame. This woodwork made it susceptible to fire, as was the case in 1720 and 1751 when blazes badly damaged the light.

In addition to aiding mariners, Boston Light protected Boston from attack. If the keeper sighted enemy ships on the horizon, he would signal the fort at Castle Island by hoisting and lowering the Union Jack as many times as there were ships approaching. The Castle would then provide a similar signal to the town. If more than four or five ships were approaching, however, the Castle fired three warning shots so that the governor could alert surrounding towns of possible attack by lighting the signal atop Beacon Hill.

If you let your imagination roam free for a moment, you can easily picture how arduous life was for the early keepers of Boston Light, many of whom had homes and farms on the harbor islands. Lightkeepers needed to do much more than just ensure that the flame remained lit through all kinds of weather. They also had to keep the lamp lenses and lantern glass clean, respond to fog signals from vessels, act as health officers in case of sickness on board incoming vessels, and occasionally entertain unexpected guests. The first guardians of the light supplemented their incomes by renting themselves out as harbor pilots, and many brave keepers risked their own lives to rescue shipwreck survivors.

Sally Snowman, Keeper of Boston Light

Sally Snowman, the seventieth keeper of Boston Light, greets visitors in eighteenth-century dress.

As a little girl growing up in Weymouth, Sally Snowman fell in love with Boston Light. As an adult, she became an auxiliary member of the U.S. Coast Guard, developing interpretive programs and writing a book on the lighthouse along with her husband. When the time came to select the seventieth keeper of Boston Light in 2003, Sally was a natural choice.

"Boston Harbor and the islands were my playground when I was growing up. We had sailboats, a powerboat, and a rowboat. I have seawater in my veins, so if I'm away from the water too long, I get very crabby. My dad brought me out to Boston Light when I was ten years old, and I instantaneously connected with it. I just knew that I'd like to get married out here one day, and in 1994 I did! The thought of being a keeper was a fantasy, and to think that my fantasy came true is phenomenal. Every day I just feel so fortunate that I'm here. I am so honored and humbled by the trust put in me to manage the oldest Coast Guard light station in the country.

"The energy of this island talks to me. It did when I was ten years old, and it still talks to me now. When you open the windows of the house, you hear the cawing of the seagulls, the bell buoys out in the harbor, and the squeal of the hydraulics from the lobstermen bringing up their traps. I keep coming out and taking pictures of the goldenrod, the monarch butterflies, and the chicory. It's just beautiful.

"Visitors come and experience the island on whatever level they want. They can look at it as a lighthouse, metaphorically the beacon of light and the salvation of the shipwrecked. Or it could just be the architecture. Others just love the concept of lighthouses and islands. So everyone is drawn to come and visit this place for various reasons. We all connect with this island."

The grave of George Worthylake, who is buried with his wife and daughter in Copp's Hill Burying Ground.

The fates of the first two keepers of Boston Light underscore the hazards of working in the outer harbor. On November 3, 1718, George Worthylake, the first keeper of Boston Light, was returning from Boston in a sloop with his family, their servant, and a friend. Near the island, Worthylake dropped anchor and the party was met by the keeper's slave, Shadwell, who had rowed out in a canoe. On their approach to the island, the canoe capsized, and everyone aboard drowned. Worthylake, his wife, and his daughter are buried underneath a triple headstone in the Copp's Hill Burying Ground in the North End. Incredibly, Worthylake's temporary replacement, Robert Saunders, drowned in stormy weather just a few days later, before his appointment was even confirmed. The terrible incident was big news in Boston, and it inspired a twelve-year-old Benjamin Franklin to write a poetic account, entitled *The Lighthouse Tragedy*, which he hawked around the docks and streets of Boston.

In the battle for American independence, Boston Light was a strategic target for both the colonists and the British. During the siege of Boston in 1775, the British still controlled the harbor and its lighthouse. On the morning of July 20, 1775, Major Joseph Vose and a detachment of colonial soldiers launched a raid on Little Brewster Island. The patriots burned the wooden parts of the lighthouse and removed three casks of oil, gunpowder, and furniture.

Protected by a guard of marines, the British quickly deployed Loyalist workers to repair Boston Light. But just eleven days after the first attack, the patriots struck again. This time, a detachment of three hundred men led by Major Benjamin Tupper landed on the island in the early morning hours. They overcame the guard and destroyed the structures being erected.

Tupper's men killed between ten and twelve British troops and made prisoners of the rest, suffering only one fatality of their own. In his General Orders of August 1, 1775, General George Washington thanked Major Tupper and his men "for their gallant and soldier-like behavior in possessing themselves of the enemy's post at the light-house and for the number of prisoners they took there."

Fast-forward to June 1776. Though the British had evacuated Boston, their ships still lurked in the harbor, where, as the October 1895 edition of the *New England Magazine* colorfully put it, they "contented themselves for a time in doing all the mischief they could upon the several islands within it." When they were finally driven from the city's waters for good on June 13, the British returned the favor. The redcoats used a timed charge to blow up the tower of Boston Light. Because of this ignominious "parting gift," the beacon at Sandy Hook, New Jersey, dating to 1764, has the distinction of being the "oldest" lighthouse structure in America. However, Bostonians can still take comfort in the fact that Boston Light remains the oldest "light station" in the United States.

Little Brewster Island remained dark for seven years before Boston Light was rebuilt under orders from Governor John Hancock in 1783. The new conical tower of brick and granite was topped by an octagonal lantern. In 1859, the tower was raised fourteen feet to accommodate a new Fresnel lens imported from France, allowing its white light to shine twenty-seven miles out to sea.

Since its earliest days, Boston Light has been a guide for thousands of sea vessels, but in September 1910 the lighthouse served as a landmark for another mode of transportation during the Harvard-Boston Aero Meet. Today, planes traveling to and from Logan Airport are familiar sights in the skies above the islands, but in 1910 few Bostonians had ever seen an airplane in person. Less than seven years after the Wright Brothers ushered in the era of flight at Kitty Hawk, the leading aviators of the world and pioneers of flight—including Wilbur Wright—gathered in Boston for only the second aviation exhibition ever held on American soil.

The meet was held at an airfield on Squantum Point across from Thompson Island. For nearly two weeks, more than one million people watched in absolute awe at the sight of these strange flying machines and the skill of the daring "bird men." Aviators vied for more than $40,000 in prize money in competitions for speed, altitude, duration, distance, landing, and even

Start of the race to Boston Light during the Harvard-Boston Aero Meet, which ran from September 3–13, 1910. Claude Grahame-White's plane is in the center, #3. *Courtesy of the Library of Congress.*

for accuracy in dropping fake bombs onto a dummy battleship. The most anticipated event, however, was the $10,000 prize put up by *The Boston Globe* for the fastest time in completing two nonstop laps from the airfield around Boston Light, a distance of thirty-three miles.

Famed English aviator Claude Grahame-White stole the show. The crowd was electric when Grahame-White, dressed in a brown canvas aviation suit, donned his head gear, adjusted his ear flaps, and mounted his machine in an attempt to make history. The engine of his monoplane hummed as he made his way down the runway and lifted off the ground, fading into the distance until he became a mere speck against the blue sky. Tens of thousands of people lined the hillsides and roofs of Hull, while passengers on a veritable fleet of boats in the harbor kept their eyes to the sky. Grahame-White passed so low over the harbor islands that it is said he scared the chickens kept on Peddocks. He then made the first of two great, wide curves around Little Brewster's tower and another lap before he returned to the airfield where the wild cheers of thousands in the grandstand and the honking horns of those watching from their automobiles greeted him. *The Boston Globe* called it the "first great race by a birdman ever seen in this part of the world." Grahame-White would complete the route a second time, and he would be the only competitor to complete the flight around Boston Light.

Two decades after the pioneers of flight whizzed above the head of the keeper of Boston Light, another winged visitor—the stork—dropped by Little Brewster Island. A doctor and a U.S. Coast Guard crew braved a nor'easter and blinding rain in the middle of the night to travel from Hull to the island to assist in the delivery of assistant keeper Ralph Norwood's seventh child, Georgia. (Two weeks prior, they faced an even fiercer storm in making the journey only to discover it was a false alarm!) The story inspired Ruth Carmen to write the novel *Storm Child*. When Georgia was five years old, she was slated to play herself in a movie version of the story. In the end, the family chose to eschew Hollywood stardom to stay at Boston Light, and the movie fell through.

At one point in the 1930s, the population of Little Brewster Island exploded to more than three keepers, their wives, and nineteen children. Sixty years later, it appeared that the island population would shrink to zero as the automation of lighthouses across the country rendered the keeper position obsolete. In actuality, Boston Light was the last lighthouse in the United States to be automated in 1998, and even then, preservation groups successfully appealed to retain a human presence on Little Brewster. To this day, Boston Light is the only remaining Coast Guard lighthouse with an official keeper.

In 2003, Sally Snowman was installed as the seventieth keeper of Boston Light—and the first female to ever hold the position. With the help of assistant lightkeepers and volunteers, Sally continues many of the rituals of her sixty-nine predecessors, such as inspecting the lighthouse lens, polishing its grass prisms, logging meteorological data, and maintaining the island's buildings. Unlike early guardians of the light, however, she also conducts seasonal tours and develops educational programs.

Massive iron doors at the base of the lighthouse, bearing the imprint of the South Boston Iron Company, open into the tower. A spiral staircase of seventy-six steps and two short ladders lead to the top of the eighty-nine-foot-tall lighthouse. Those who scale the tower come face-to-face with the giant two-ton Fresnel lens, which was installed in 1859 and is eleven feet tall and dotted with 336 twelve-sided glass prisms that resemble a kaleidoscope. The view from the top of the lighthouse is a magnificent panorama of the harbor, its islands, the open Atlantic, and the Boston skyline nearly ten miles away.

A small vestibule at the base of the lighthouse functions as a museum that includes lighthouse artifacts and early navigation aids. The most prized possession—and the Coast Guard's oldest artifact—is the station's fog cannon that dates back to 1719. Keepers fired the cannon to answer blasts from ships that found themselves blanketed in by the fog. A fog bell replaced the cannon in 1851, and a siren was added in the 1880s. A bell similar to the one used at Boston Light stands outside the entrance to the lighthouse tower.

In preparation of Boston Light's 2016 tricentennial, the Coast Guard embarked on a $1.5 million facelift of the light station. When workers refreshed the beacon's mortar and repointed its granite blocks, they discovered a surprise hidden underneath the white stucco exterior—the tower's original 1716 foundation. The granite stones that formed the lighthouse's

Little Brewster Island circa 1906. *Courtesy of the Library of Congress, Detroit Publishing Company Collection.*

foundation had apparently survived the British destruction, although they had turned a cherry pink color from the stress of the explosion.

In addition to the lighthouse tower, there are five other whitewashed structures on Little Brewster Island, including an engine house, boathouse, cistern building, and oil house, all which date from the nineteenth century. Perched on top of the rocky ledges, these gable-roofed buildings give the appearance of a tiny New England fishing village. There are no shrubs or trees, and most of the island is covered by a green lawn and colorful wildflowers in the summer and early fall. Cormorants and gulls roost on the island's rocky ledges and fish the nearby waters.

The keeper's house, with an American flag proudly flying in front, dates from 1884. The two-story house has high ceilings, hardwood floors, and large windows that let in the light. This white clapboard house could be just about any old New England home—except for the venerable lighthouse that continues to stand watch right outside its door.

ADDITIONAL INFORMATION

At the time of publication, Little Brewster Island is closed due to storm-related damage. A two-hour, narrated lighthouse cruise that sails past Boston Light as well as Graves Light and Long Island Light runs on weekends between June and September. Tickets cost $35 for adults; $30 for students, seniors, and military; $25 for kids; and free for kids three and under. The hope is to resume tours of Little Brewster Island that provide visitors a chance to scale Boston Light. For the latest information on Boston Light tours and access to Little Brewster Island for private boaters, visit bostonharborislands.org or call (617) 223-8666.

"To the merchants of Boston this view of the lighthouse . . ." A reproduction of a mezzotint from 1729 by William Burgis. *Courtesy of the Library of Congress.*

Seawall ruins litter the coast of Great Brewster Island.

Great Brewster Island

THE MASSIVE ESCARPMENT OF GREAT BREWSTER ISLAND is one of the most recognizable landmarks in Boston Harbor. The island's northern bluff, weather-beaten and scarred from thousands of years of the ocean's abuse, has eroded into a sheer cliff of sand. For generations of Boston mariners, the northern bluff of Great Brewster Island has been a welcome sign that they were nearly home. For boats leaving the Boston waterfront, it's a familiar pointer toward open waters.

At over one hundred feet high, the bluff on Great Brewster is striking even from miles away. That it becomes even more awe-inspiring as you navigate along its shoreline is one of Mother Nature's pleasant tricks. Looking up at the cliff from the surface of the harbor, it feels as if you are at the bottom of a canyon and a giant claw has taken a swipe at the island's side. Whole sections of the bluff have been lost to landslides and washed away with the tide. The ridges that have formed along the side of the cliff offer a

Great Brewster Island's weather-beaten northern bluff has been eroded into a sheer cliff of sand.

lovely interplay of light and shadows changing as the sun moves across the sky, with the most picturesque colors emerging at sunset. The view is just as scenic when you alight onto the island and scale the summit of its northern bluff, the highest point in the outer harbor. It can be a bit of a workout, but the payoff is worth it. The water of the outer harbor sparkles, and if you listen closely, you can hear the cries of the cormorants on nearby Shag Rocks.

As the largest island in the outer harbor at nearly seventy acres at low tide, Great Brewster is filled with both natural and man-made wonders that can entertain for hours. Hiking trails and mowed paths make it easy to wander across the island, and numerous picnic tables provide plenty of opportunities to relax and enjoy the surroundings. Unfortunately, the dock has been washed away, so there is no longer public ferry service to the island. Do not let this deter you; kayaks and flat-bottomed boats can land on the island's western beach, and staging a beach landing is well worth it.

The Brewsters (Great Brewster, Little Brewster, Middle Brewster, and Outer Brewster Islands) are said to be named in honor of Elder William Brewster, the spiritual leader of the Pilgrims. Brewster, the first preacher and teacher of the Plymouth Bay Colony, played a major role in planning and organizing the voyage of the *Mayflower* to America.

Naming these islands after a Pilgrim who sought safe harbor in America is apt, since the Brewsters ensure the safety of Boston Harbor. These rugged, windswept islands form a natural breakwater, shielding the inner harbor from the wrath of the open ocean. The other islands in the Brewster chain are outcroppings of bedrock, giving them the strength to weather such wicked conditions. Great Brewster, however, is a drumlin island created by glacial deposits of clay and gravel, and that softer geological composition makes it more vulnerable to erosion. Completely exposed to easterly gales, the island has borne the brunt of nature's fury for thousands of years.

By the middle of the nineteenth century, eroded material from the island began to fill up the shipping channel and posed a considerable threat to commerce. As a result, the federal government in 1848 began construction of a massive seawall to protect the island and the channel. The enormous granite blocks of the seawall around the north and south heads and along the eastern shore of Great Brewster Island remain today. Sections of the seawall are still intact, but decades of ravaging waves have taken their toll and some portions are now in disrepair. Be sure to heed the "No Trespassing" signs where they are posted.

In some sections, the mighty sea has smashed through the gray slabs of granite as if they were mere building blocks. Crumbled stretches of the seawall have given birth to thriving tidal pools among the rocks. The tidal pools support mussels, snails, starfish, and crabs as well as lichens and barnacles. This convenient supply of food sustains a colony of gulls on the island. It's a common sight to look above and see the skies filled with gulls, their wings spread as they glide through the air. The east side of the island, along the seawall, is a breeding ground in the early summer for herring (gray-winged) and great black-backed (black-winged) gulls. Young gulls usually hatch in June and take flight by August. Gulls are very protective of their young during nesting and rearing season and might swoop aggressively to scare unwanted intruders away, so it's wise to keep your distance at those times of the year.

The middle portion of state-owned Great Brewster Island is dominated by a salt marsh, which can be inundated in stormy weather and during the winter, but dries up in the summer months. This area of the island is relatively devoid of sumac groves and trees, which allows for a fantastic, unencumbered panorama of Boston Harbor. Looking west, the skyscrapers of downtown Boston and the egg digesters of Deer Island rise above the grasses and cattails growing in the marsh. Turning to the east, the stately white pillar of Boston Light, less than a half mile away, soars above the seawall.

Shutterbugs will be pleased by the exceptional snapshots they'll be able to get from this vantage point.

With Great Brewster and Little Brewster Islands separated by only a shallow sandbar, the keepers of Boston Light often traveled to Great Brewster. George Worthylake, the first keeper of Boston Light, is said to have grazed sheep on Great Brewster, and for many years, a well on the island supplied keepers of Boston Light with drinking water. During the 1700s and 1800s, in addition to grazing livestock, Great Brewster Island was used to supply stone and gravel ballast for thousands of ships, which no doubt helped contribute to its wearing away.

By the latter half of the nineteenth century, Great Brewster Island became home to a handful of summer residents. Benjamin Dean, who owned Outer Brewster Island and served in the U.S. House of Representatives, moved his summer villa to the island sometime around 1875. The island was also a seasonal home for fishermen, and by the 1930s, about a dozen families had summer cottages on the island. Sporadic stone wall foundations and remnants of plants cultivated by residents, such as asparagus and Concord grapes, can still be spotted on the island.

The cottage community came to an end with the outbreak of World War II. To help protect the city, the federal government took over the island, which held strategic importance at the entrance to Boston Harbor. The U.S. Army deployed 120 soldiers from Fort Strong on Long Island to Great Brewster Island, and the new military reservation included a mess hall, barracks, post exchange, and pump house.

The military placed a battery of ninety-millimeter rapid-fire guns on the northern bluff to ward off torpedo boats. It also stationed anti-aircraft guns, observation posts, and searchlights on the island, but Great Brewster's primary use was as a command post that assisted in controlling the electronically operated minefields in Boston Harbor. A bomb- and gas-proof bunker, burrowed into the island's south hill, was filled with electronic equipment to assist Fort Dawes on Deer Island with the operation of mines along the north channel of Boston Harbor. Signals were transmitted from an observation constructed on top.

Unfortunately, World War II was not the first time that Great Brewster Island was touched by armed conflict. Massachusetts General Court records indicate that Great Brewster Island was used as an internment site for Native Americans during King Philip's War. A November 1675 order

The westward view from Great Brewster Island to the Boston skyline.

Great Brewster Island offers wonderful views for a picnic.

directed Native American women who chose not to join their husbands in prison or on Deer Island be sent to Great Brewster Island. A few months later, the General Court compensated colonists who owned the island for its use in confining the Native Americans.

Many of the military buildings built during World War II were removed after its conclusion, but some concrete foundations of the buildings and platforms for the searchlights and gun batteries can still be seen today. The shell of the bunker in the south hill also remains, but there is little to see other than its bare concrete walls. Exploration is unadvisable as the bunker is dark and contains asbestos. What's much more enjoyable is a walk along the sweeping, rocky beaches below its entrance.

Walking south along the beach leads to the Great Brewster Spit, extending from the southwestern tip of the island. The spit is exposed at low tide, and though it may look inviting for the adventurous explorer, tidal currents and slippery rocks can make it extremely dangerous.

The arched breakwater snakes for nearly a mile before it ends near Lovells Island at the entrance to the Narrows Channel, once the main shipping route to Boston. For more than seventy years, an odd-looking red lighthouse stood guard at the end of the bar as a warning to mariners of the hidden danger. The Narrows Light, erected in 1856, was in reality a dwelling with its roof cut to allow its warning beacon to be seen. The wooden, hexagonal structure was perched thirty-five feet high above the sea on seven spindly iron stilts, which gave it the appearance of a huge water insect and earned it the endearing nickname of "Bug Light."

On the morning of June 7, 1929, keeper Thomas Small was using a blowtorch to remove paint from the outside walls of Bug Light when suddenly a portion of the wall above his head caught fire. Winds fed the flames, which overtook the lighthouse in just minutes. Small barely escaped before Bug Light collapsed into the harbor, launching sea spray high into the air. All that remained was a twisted mess of iron.

After wandering the rugged terrain of Great Brewster, you'll no doubt be hungry. A set of picnic tables on the crest of the island's southern hill above the spit is the perfect place for a picnic. Face one way toward the city or face the other toward Boston Light. It's a setting that captures the essence of the outer harbor islands: an extraordinary ocean wilderness teetering between the open waters to the east and the bustling city to the west.

Native American History on the Boston Harbor Islands

A few thousand years after the end of the last Ice Age, Native Americans began to populate the drumlins of the Boston Harbor Islands that were left behind by the retreating glaciers. Stone tools and pottery unearthed by archaeologists on Long Island date back as far as nine thousand years. The Native Americans who lived seasonally on the islands sustained themselves through light agriculture and by clamming, fishing, hunting waterfowl, and gathering fruits, nuts, and berries. Shell middens excavated on a number of the islands have revealed that ducks, codfish, clams, and sturgeon were staples of the diets of Native Americans who inhabited the islands.

When English explorer John Smith sailed into Boston Harbor in 1614, he witnessed a thriving indigenous population along its shores, describing "many isles all planted with corn, groves, mulberries, savage gardens, and good harbors." He also wrote, "the seacoast, as you pass, shows you all along large corn-fields and great troops of well-proportioned people."

Upon his return a mere six years later, however, Smith discovered that Native American populations had been decimated by diseases likely brought by Europeans to New England. "Where I had seen one hundred or two hundred people [in 1614], there is scarce ten to be found," Smith reported. When Englishman Thomas Morton settled on the shoreline of Boston Harbor in the 1620s, he encountered an apocalyptic landscape that he compared to a "new-found Golgatha" where bodies of the dead "were left for crows, kites, and vermin to prey upon."

A half century later, colonists and Native Americans across southern New England took up arms against each other, and the Boston Harbor Islands played a particularly dark chapter in the story of King Philip's War. On August 30, 1675, the Massachusetts Bay Colony ordered the confinement and resettlement of all Native Americans—including those who had converted to Christianity and pledged their loyalty to English rule—to five villages in present-day Natick, Canton, Littleton, Lowell, and Grafton. Any Native Americans found outside those villages in the colony could be legally shot on sight.

Two months later, the Massachusetts Bay Colony began to forcibly remove Native Americans from those villages to Deer Island, where they were given no shelter, little protection from freezing temperatures, and limited food supplies. Long and Great Brewster Islands were later used to intern Native Americans as well. By February 1676, the internment villages on the mainland had largely been abandoned. Its remaining occupants had either escaped the English zone of control, been killed, or been removed to the Boston Harbor Islands where they were joined by prisoners of war captured by the colonists.

The exact number of Native Americans imprisoned on the Boston Harbor Islands and the count of those who died from starvation, exposure, and illness during the winter of 1675–1676 is unknown—but it is believed to be in the hundreds, if not thousands. That history makes the islands sacred spaces for many Native Americans. "Descendants are concerned about what happened to their ancestors and how those sites are being treated today," says Gary McCann, a policy adviser for both the Muhheconneuk Intertribal Committee on Deer Island and the Muhheconnew National Confederacy Bureau of Political Affairs. "We don't have a clear history of what exactly that looks like because the colonists did not lay out exact numbers of deaths."

Also unknown is the location of the burial grounds of Native Americans held captive on the islands. When the city of Boston in 2018 proposed the reconstruction of the Long Island Bridge, local tribes voiced their concern about the potential for the project to disturb burial grounds. "The identification of sites has never taken place," McCann says. "The lack of identification makes it ambiguous about whether new construction would impact those sites or not.

"There's a lot of information that still needs to be filled in," McCann says. "That's why it's important to be cautious with any use of the islands, to ensure any remains can be preserved. If you destroy the evidence, particularly given the absence of a written record, it's hard to have a more fully developed picture of what happened out there."

Middle Brewster Island

NO AMERICAN CITY HAS STRONGER IRISH ROOTS than Boston, and no landscape in metropolitan Boston is more evocative of the Emerald Isle than Middle Brewster Island. The cliffs, the pounding Atlantic surf, the stone walls, and the crumbling ruins strewn across a field of windswept grass offer the same blend of raw and rugged wilderness that lures so many to Ireland's romantic shores.

In the center of this wild and untamed landscape is an old arch, standing ten feet high. When viewed from just the right perspective, the lichen-coated archway perfectly frames the distant Boston skyline. Once the entrance to the white brick villa that commanded a cliff on the island's southwest corner, the arch is little more than a relic from a time when Middle Brewster was a summer retreat for some of Boston's most prominent citizens.

The first of these notable Bostonians who spent their summers on thirteen-acre Middle Brewster Island was Augustus Russ, the founder of the Boston Yacht Club and one of the city's best-known lawyers. Russ purchased the island in 1871 and leased several lots to other residents, including millionaire Benjamin P. Cheney and his wife, Julia Arthur. Before the couple built their palatial estate on neighboring Calf Island, they lived on Middle Brewster in a more modest home, The Capstan.

Russ enjoyed spending his summer days and nights in solitude on Middle Brewster while commuting daily to and from Boston in his yacht. After Russ passed away in 1892, one of his law partners, Melvin O. Adams, purchased the island. One of the most-celebrated lawyers in Massachusetts, Adams served as an assistant district attorney in Suffolk County, a district attorney for the federal government, and also president of the Boston, Revere Beach & Lynn Railroad. His great fame, however, came from his role on the defense team during the 1893 trial of the infamous Lizzie Borden, who was accused and acquitted of hacking her father and stepmother to death with an ax. One paper of the time described Adams as "the eyes, the ears, and the directing hand of the defense."

Sharing the island with these Gilded Age figures was a colony of fishermen and their families, who began living on Middle Brewster Island in

the middle of the nineteenth century. One of these humble cottages was the scene of a very bizarre—and tragic—fatality in 1923. On a June morning, Victor Ciarmataro joined his father and brother on a motorboat trip from their home in the North End to the Brewsters to harvest periwinkles. After a few hours of work, the thirsty teenager knocked on the door of the home of the island's caretaker, Hjalmar Roos, for a drink. Getting no answer, the boy went around to the window on the back porch and found it unlocked.

Chuck Zonderman. *Nicole L. Vecchiotti.*

Chuck's Tips for Fishing Boston Harbor

Following his time in the service and before becoming dockmaster at Hingham Shipyard Marinas, Chuck Zonderman was a commercial lobsterman for thirty years. When he wasn't working, he was pleasure boating—few people are as knowledgeable as he about fishing Boston Harbor.

"When it comes to fishing, knowing the types of water different fish like is half the battle. Using the correct bait accounts for most of the other half.

"Early fall is the time to go bass fishing, though they're around as early as April. Flocks of birds feeding on bait fish are a good indication they're around. Look around river mouths for early bass. (Try the Back River and the Fore River.) Bigger bass come into the harbor in search of the warm water found in the deeper channels. A popular rig to use is a tube and worm. Chunking works well, too. Anchor your boat and let the bait drift down tide.

"These days, codfish are not as prevalent in the spring, though we'll see them later into the fall. You'll find rock cod around Point Allerton and Boston Light, and larger ocean cod around the B-buoy, Thieves Ledge off Hull, and Graves and Minot's Light. Cod prefer clams to sea worms. A weighted lure with a treble hook, or a cod jig works well.

"In the late fall, the flounder start showing up. Flounder are soft-bottom fish. They dig in the mud for the winter. By early December, they're pretty much dormant. Try around Peddocks, Rainsford, Long, and Green Islands—or anywhere there's soft bottom, even in shallow water. Flounder return in the spring, when the water starts to warm. By mid-summer, they're only found offshore. They're great eating fish and sea worms tend to be the best bait.

"Bluefish are a warmer water fish than cod. They come through in the early summer, chasing poagies in a frenzy. Like mackerel, bluefish can be caught while they are feeding near the surface of the water. Blues (and big bass) are also out in the deeper water around the B-buoy and can be caught both on the surface and deeper down. Bluefish and bass are readily caught as far in as Wollaston Beach. Good spots for mackerel are Harding's Ledge off of Nantasket, the Bay off Pemberton, and A Street in Hull on the bayside.

"We used to see haddock around Graves Light, but these days you have to go further into open water. There's some small tuna fishing offshore. Occasionally you'll see them around Minot's Ledge or inside the B-buoy. (You'll also see whales and dolphin just to the east of these offshore ledges.) Outside the Brewster Islands, you might find some good size sharks, too."

Victor decided to open the window, which, unfortunately, proved to be a deadly decision. Roos, plagued by thefts while he was out fishing, had booby-trapped the window so that a rifle would fire. As soon as Victor pushed up the sash, he was shot in the stomach. The caretaker pled guilty to manslaughter, but he was only fined $750 since the boy was ruled to have been breaking and entering. Eight years later, Roos was ordered to pay civil damages of $6,000. The descendants of Melvin Adams paid both fines, and Roos continued to live on the island, serving as its caretaker.

These days, birds are the primary residents of state-owned Middle Brewster Island, and a small freshwater marsh on the eastern side attracts a wide variety. Rookeries for two species of herons are found on the island's southeast corner, and it is a nesting site for gulls and cormorants. Visitation is greatly discouraged during nesting time.

Middle Brewster is an untamed ocean wilderness, and even for the most experienced adventurer, exploring this island can be dangerous. Access is understandably (though regrettably) discouraged. The cliffs, nearly perpendicular in spots, and the sunken crags that surround the island make it rather complicated to get ashore. And there are few beaches and inlets on which to land, making it the most inaccessible of the Brewsters. The interior of the island is equally challenging to navigate. There are no trails to follow, and thickets are a constant impediment.

Still, Middle Brewster is possibly the most beautiful and romantic island in Boston Harbor—in no small part because of the house foundations, crumbling fireplaces, and stone walls that once demarcated the island's properties. Though they are now weathered and overgrown, these ruins provide mystical clues as to how this terrain once looked when the summer colony thrived. And, of course, there is the arch. Luckily, it is just as lovely from the water.

Arthur Austin's unfinished channel nearly divided Outer Brewster into two islands.
Nicole L. Vecchiotti.

Outer Brewster Island

FROM THE WEATHER-BEATEN CLIFFS on the eastern side of Outer Brewster Island all that separates you from Spain is three thousand miles of open ocean.

Remote Outer Brewster isn't just at the outermost reaches of the national park area, it is also the most threatened by human activity. It began when Nathaniel Austin Jr., Middlesex County sheriff and state senator, quarried rock from the island's shores for the city's buildings and street pavement. In the 1820s, stone removed from Outer Brewster was used to construct the three-story Austin Block, which still stands at 92 Main Street in Charlestown near the historic Warren Tavern. When the Austin Block was renovated in the 1980s, stone was again harvested from Outer Brewster to restore the first floor. Outer Brewster's stone also paved the Warren Bridge, which connected Charlestown to the North End. (Law students might recall the construction of the bridge led to the famous 1837 case *Charles River Bridge v. Warren Bridge* that was argued before the U.S. Supreme Court.)

According to some historical accounts, Nathaniel Austin's brother, Arthur, who was deeded the island in the 1840s, attempted to cut a narrow channel through the island's solid rock so that boats could find refuge in stormy weather. A lengthy canal was excavated, but this particular "big dig" was never completed. The channel, which nearly divides the island in two, remains today.

During the nineteenth century, Bostonians took advantage of Outer Brewster Island's seclusion to engage in activities that were frowned upon within the city limits, such as illegal boxing matches. One such bout, which *The Boston Democrat* referred to as "one of these disgusting and brutal exhibitions," occurred in 1844. Under the cover of darkness, pugilists Joe Long and an Englishman named Smith—along with two hundred spectators—set sail from Boston at

Nicole L. Vecchiotti.

2:00 a.m. The fight, which finally began at 9:00 a.m., lasted two hours and one hundred rounds before Long emerged victorious. *The Boston Democrat* was outraged and hoped "the parties to this most disgraceful affair" would be appropriately punished.

Outer Brewster's relatively barren landscape and rocky shoreline made the island essentially uninhabitable, although a small group of fishermen and lobstermen did reside there in the latter half of the nineteenth century. By the time the federal government purchased the island in 1913 (for a mere $2,500), there was just a single fisherman living on its shores.

The government bought the island in the name of coastal defense, but it wasn't fortified until 1942, after the outbreak of World War II. The Outer Brewster Military Reservation included a six-inch shielded gun emplacement, three barracks capable of housing 125 men, a mess hall, a desalinization plant, and a long-range radar unit mounted on a one-hundred-foot tower.

Today, the ruins of the military reservation, deactivated after World War II, are prominent on the middle and western end of the island. The gray concrete shells of the barracks, now surrounded by a maze of sumac, occupy the island's western bluffs. Surely, there were few soldiers during the war who had a better view than the ones who lived in the barracks on Outer Brewster.

The circular gun batteries, the base of the radar tower, and the entrance to Battery Jewell are impossible to miss. Built beneath the island's highest crest, the battery served as a bomb- and chemical-proof bunker. Entering the

tunnels and abandoned ammunition rooms inside the battery and barracks is discouraged, and generally visitors should take care to avoid any unmarked and uncovered wells and pits that remain from the island's military days.

Some well-trodden paths on parts of the twenty-acre island make it easier to hike Outer Brewster than the other islands in the outer harbor, but the high bluffs and rocky shoreline make Outer Brewster equally difficult to access. During rough weather, the island is virtually unapproachable.

If the tide is right, however, a small rocky cove on the island's northern shore offers a good spot for dinghies or kayaks to come ashore. To the east of the cove is the fissure that remains from Arthur Austin's abandoned plans to build an artificial harbor. Even if the channel is dry, some rock scaling is required to cross to the island's eastern end.

Just to the west of the cove, along the island's northern shore, is the island's most unique natural geological form—Pulpit Rock, named for its resemblance to a minister's podium. When the wind blows across this tall, tabletop formation it sounds as if Mother Nature herself is shaking the rock, ferociously declaring her almighty power.

Since Outer Brewster Island is so windswept and exposed to the elements, only a small stand of quaking aspens can be found. Much of the island is covered with tall grass and staghorn sumac, which is thickest around the military ruins. What the island lacks in flora it makes up for in fauna, and Outer Brewster supports one of the most diverse collections of

breeding water birds in Boston Harbor. The island provides a nesting habitat for coastal waterbirds such as cormorants, wading birds, waterfowl, shorebirds, and gulls. American oystercatchers and common eider ducks nest on the island, and ibis have been spotted as well. As birds can be aggressive during nesting season, access is discouraged at that time.

The cleanup of Boston Harbor has revitalized the aquatic wildlife around Outer Brewster Island as well. By the 1980s, pollution made the harbor devoid of the biodiversity that attracts large marine animals, such as seals and porpoises. Now that smelt, herring, and mackerel populations have rebounded, the seals and porpoises have returned. White and brown seals can be seen on the rocks of Outer Brewster and the nearby islands, more so in the wintertime. Also, thanks to the harbor cleanup, the water around Outer Brewster offers the best scuba diving around Boston.

Arthur Austin's designs for an artificial harbor may have left a permanent scar on Outer Brewster, but other development plans hatched over the years could have obliterated the island's landscape altogether. In the 1960s and 1970s, propositions to fill in the harbor between the Brewsters to build a trash dump, recreation area, and even an airport were considered. More recently, power conglomerate AES Corporation proposed construction of a $500 million import and storage facility for liquefied natural gas on Outer Brewster in 2006. The proposal called for blasting out the interior of the state-owned island to build two tanks, each one hundred feet deep, and restricting access to fishing and boating around the island. Thankfully, the plan died after an intense fight by a coalition of environmental organizations and island lovers. However, it stands as a distressing example of the threat that continues to face the Boston Harbor Islands—and, in particular, this most remote of isles.

The view looking out from Battery Jewell on Outer Brewster Island.

The Birds of the Boston Harbor Islands

Since the Boston Harbor Islands national park area provides a habitat for a significant number of colonial-nesting waterbirds, it has been designated as an Important Bird Area. The park's variety of habitats (marine, rock cliff, beach, salt marsh, and forest) support over two hundred bird species, according to field surveys. Those species include ducks, geese, hawks, gulls, terns, herons, owls, woodpeckers, doves, sandpipers, and plovers.

Many species of waterbirds nest on the islands. It is common to see large colonies of double-crested cormorants, herring gulls, great black-backed gulls, and common eider ducks on the rocky shores and scrub habitats of the outer islands. Black-crowned night herons, snowy egrets, great egrets, and to a lesser extent, glossy ibis, breed among the islands as well. These wading birds

nest in the trees along the coastlines. As suspected, smaller islands have less diverse populations of breeding landbirds than larger islands. Landbirds such as song sparrows and yellow warblers are common to the area.

Migrating shorebirds are most commonly found in the refuges of mudflats and salt marshes on Snake, Rainsford, Thompson, and the Brewster Islands from

July through August. In the past, sightings have included black-bellied plovers and ruddy turnstones. Flocks of waterfowl are drawn to the islands in late fall and winter, and snowy owls and bald eagles have been spotted in wintertime. Keep a sharp eye, and you might even spot the red knot, which migrates over nine thousand miles between South America and the Arctic and makes occasional rest stops among the islands.

Park managers use the size of the breeding bird populations and the number of nests, eggs, and chicks to gauge the environmental health of the park. Breeding season occurs from May through the end of July. The public is asked to respect this delicate stage in the life cycle and not to disturb the colonies while they are at work.

(Top left to bottom right) Ruddy turnstone (*ps50ace/Getty Images*), purple sandpiper (*MikeLane45/Getty Images*), female eider (*Dgwildlife/Getty Images*); Snowy egret (*ps50ace/Getty Images*), lesser yellowlegs (*impr2003/Getty Images*), piping plover (*bephotographers/Getty Images*).

A freshwater pond sits in the center of Calf Island.

Calf Island

THE REDBRICK CHIMNEY TOWERING OVER the landscape of Calf Island stands testament to a bygone era when the islands served as personal retreats for some of Boston's wealthiest residents. Today, sumacs sprout from the foundation that once supported the palatial summer home of millionaire railroad financier Benjamin P. Cheney Jr. and the beautiful Shakespearean stage actress and silent film star Julia Arthur. Built in 1902 after the couple moved from Middle Brewster Island, their estate, The Moorings, would have been equally at home among the mansions of Newport.

The Moorings dominated the crest of thirty-five-acre Calf Island, facing west toward Boston and commanding a broad sweep of the sea on all sides. *The Boston Globe* described it as the "first beauty touch to be given to one of the gaunt, inhospitable-looking Brewster islands." The two-story home was gigantic—twenty rooms in all—and lavishly decorated with solid-oak furniture and hard-pine ceilings and floors. Photographs and paintings adorned the exquisite cypress-paneled walls. Outside, a stone veranda ran along three sides of the house.

With a half dozen guest rooms in their mansion, the Cheneys were constantly entertaining. Their guests must have spent hours soaking in the glorious panorama from the stone belvedere built on the precipitous cliff in front of the house, below which Benjamin Cheney docked his steam launch and yacht. Eight servants tended to the property, and a large boathouse included their sleeping and living quarters.

The Cheneys planned to add a swimming pool and golf links to the estate, but those plans never came to fruition. Instead, the couple's carefree days on Calf Island came to an abrupt end in a stunning reversal of fortune when Cheney, who had inherited $10 million, shocked the city by declaring bankruptcy in 1917. Three years later, the treasures of The Moorings were picked over by prospective buyers at auction. Julia Arthur, who had vowed never to act again when she moved to Calf Island, was forced to return to the stage.

The government ended up seizing Calf Island and The Moorings by eminent domain for military use at the onset of World War I, and over the decades the estate fell victim to fire and vandals. (Cheney himself met a strange death in 1942 when he apparently died of dehydration in an Arizona desert—an ironic end for a man who spent glorious summers at the water's edge.)

It seems Calf Island was always fit for kings and queens. Decades before the Cheneys arrived, a small colony of lobstermen and fishermen lived on Calf Island. Their humble cottages couldn't have been more different from The Moorings—and no Calf Island resident was more salty or eccentric than James J. Turner, the anointed "King of Calf Island."

Turner, a lobsterman, moved to Calf Island in the 1840s and lived there for nearly forty years until he passed away at ninety. He was a wild and unkempt man, and an illustration of Turner in his later years depicts him as weather-beaten and gaunt, with a long white beard hiding his face. Rumors swirled that the King had been a pirate and murderer in a previous life.

The "palace" from which the King of Calf Island reigned was a modest cottage that included the chartroom and pilot house from the wrecked steamer *Ontario*, which Turner had towed over from Apple Island. He lived in the cottage with his son, James E. Turner, who was six years old when his father brought him to Calf Island. The elder Turner, a strict disciplinarian, forced his son to perform military drills with a rifle for hours on end. On Sundays, the King would review the drills while dressed in a Turkish outfit that included a red sash and fez. Despite this strange upbringing, James E. Turner developed an affinity for Calf Island, too. He lived there for more than fifty years, and in true dynastic succession, the son became known as the "Emperor of Calf Island."

The fishermen who lived on the island, including the Turners, courageously rescued shipwreck survivors and buried the victims in unmarked graves at the top of the island. According to historical accounts, the primitive graveyard contains the remains of twenty-one sailors lost in nearby waters. The conditions around Calf Island were so treacherous that the Massachusetts Humane Society built one of its first huts of refuge on its southwest coast in 1789.

Calf Island has seen a wide range of uses over the centuries. There is evidence that Native Americans occupied the island seasonally, and the island was used to pasture livestock by early European settlers. In the late nineteenth century, Bostonians spent summer Sundays recreating on the island, and there were frequent reports of illicit boxing matches on the Sabbath. While the federal government acquired the rights to Calf Island in 1917, it didn't see much military activity until World War II, when it was home to a small garrison that manned an advanced anti-aircraft searchlight, radar, and observation site.

Today, there are no remains of the military reservation and little signs of previous human activity other than the ruins of The Moorings and a few cultivars, such as cherry trees and mock orange shrubs. The majority of Calf Island is covered by grasses, sumacs, and some salt-tolerant trees.

Julia Arthur, queen of the stage, vowed never to act again once she and her husband moved to Calf Island from Middle Brewster. *Courtesy of the Library of Congress.*

Calf Island has several beaches where visitors can come ashore in a dinghy or kayak. One of the better landing spots is in a sandy cove on the island's western shore. If the water is too rough on the west side of the island, a rocky but protected beach on the island's east side offers another option. Several unimproved trails run along the west shore of Calf Island leading to the ruins of The Moorings, but overall the island is difficult to traverse. At its center is a freshwater pond surrounded by tidal marshes.

Most visitors to Calf Island, now owned by the state, are drawn to the ruins of Benjamin P. Cheney's house and that lone chimney—the last of the estate's five great fireplaces.

Julia Arthur's monogram was inlaid in the dining room fireplace, which is now gone. The remaining chimney, which heated the billiards room, still boasts Cheney's initials, "BP," fashioned from white sea pebbles. All it takes is a little imagination to feel the hardwood floors beneath your feet, see the summer breeze ruffling the drapes, and hear the voice of old B.P. telling you to "Rack 'em!"

The view toward Outer Brewster.
Nicole L. Vecchiotti.

Little Calf Island

LITTLE CALF ISLAND IS JUST OVER one hundred yards north of its big brother, Calf Island. At low tide the two islands might seem as though they are connected, and at one time they probably were. The shallow passage between is rife with hidden ledges and shoals. Mariners should take extreme caution if they attempt to pass between the islands.

Little Calf Island is tiny, desolate, and devoid of vegetation. In 1835, the owner of Little Calf Island tried to lease the tiny bedrock outcrop on the implausible proposition that it was ideally suited to pasturing sheep or a fishing camp. Even though centuries of Poseidon's fury have likely reduced the island to its diminutive size—Little Calf weighs in at less than an acre—these selling points were for the birds. Literally.

The state-owned island is a nesting site for herring gulls, black-backed gulls, and cormorants. It's not unusual to find hundreds of birds perched on the surf-beaten rocks. Alas, even if you did want to explore this rugged landscape, there is no safe place to land. Luckily, the on-water views are just as good.

Sherman "Pat" Morss Jr.

Green Island

NORTH OF LITTLE CALF ISLAND is rocky Green Island, the two islands separated by the swift-flowing waters of Hypocrite Channel. On early maps, Green Island was labeled as "North Brewster Island." According to some historical accounts of the islands, Green Island received its current name from Joseph Green, a colonial Boston merchant said to have owned the island at one time.

The islands in Boston Harbor certainly attracted their fair share of nonconformists, and Green Island was no exception. It was home to the recluse Samuel Choate, who built a rudimentary hut made of driftwood in 1845 and lived on the island for twenty years, subsisting on fish, lobster, and the mussels he harvested around the islands. *The Boston Journal* described Choate as a "hermit of somewhat singular habits and possessing a very independent spirit." (One begs to ask if that isn't true of all hermits.)

Despite the miserable, harsh winters Choate must have endured, he remained on that bleak island until he was nearly seventy years of age, when he was finally induced by the Harbor Police to return to civilization. Shortly after leaving the island, Choate passed away in a Bridgewater almshouse.

Through the 1800s and into the early 1900s, fishermen and lobstermen lived in shanties on Green Island, but today there are no traces of this community on the island, which is less than three acres at high tide. With little soil and plant life, the state-owned island is a refuge and nesting spot for gulls, cormorants, and other birds. Beaches are lacking on Green Island, and the rocky ledges

surrounding the island make landing difficult and dangerous. Accordingly, public access to Green Island is discouraged, particularly during nesting season when birds can be aggressive.

Shermann"Pat" Morss Jr.

Shag Rocks

FROM AFAR, THEY APPEAR AS TINY LITTLE DOTS on the rocks protruding from the sea, but as you draw closer, the shapes begin to take form, revealing a scene reminiscent of Alfred Hitchcock's movie *The Birds*. Dozens of cormorants and gulls roost on the bedrock ledges of the curiously named Shag Rocks. (The name makes more sense once you know that cormorants were known as "shags" to the British settlers in Boston.)

Although it's less than a half-mile northeast of Boston Light, Shag Rocks has seen its fair share of shipwrecks, and on numerous occasions the keepers of Boston Light launched rescues for vessels that had run aground on the craggy outcropping. The worst of these wrecks, and one of the most tragic marine disasters ever to happen in Boston Harbor, occurred when a great gale rammed the square-rigger

Maritana into Shag Rocks just after midnight on November 3, 1861. The powerful storm, which drove the tides above the wharves of the Boston waterfront and nearly to the doors of the Custom House, lodged the *Maritana* between two massive rocks. The crew was forced to cut the masts in attempt to save the ship.

Many dark hours passed without salvation. Shortly after dawn broke, so did the mighty ship. It split in two and plunged twenty-six of the passengers and crew, including women and children, to their deaths. Thirteen people clung tenaciously to the rocks until they were rescued by lifesavers from Hull, nearly twelve hours after their ordeal began. The November 5, 1861, edition of the *Boston Journal* reported: "A more complete wreck was never seen . . . God save us all from a death like this."

Clearly, Shag Rocks can be a perilous place to approach, and access by boat is impractical. However, while they are a menace to boaters, the large crags and boulders scattered for nearly a third of a mile across Shag Rocks create a great lobster-diving and fishing spot for striped bass, flounder, and mackerel—a fact the birds have known for years.

The Graves

IT'S EASY TO FEEL SORRY FOR GRAVES LIGHT. Even though it's taller and more powerful than Boston Light, Graves Light is often lost in the shadow of its older sibling. Every year, tourists flock to Boston Light, lured by its history and quintessential New England charm. Boston Light even has its own keeper. And Graves Light gets none of this attention.

Truth be told, Graves Light is more imposing than welcoming, and when the fog rolls in, the light can appear downright eerie and haunting. (When the producers of the 1948 motion picture *A Portrait of Jennie* needed a forlorn lighthouse for the climax of their film, they chose Graves Light.) Yet, there is an undeniable majesty to this austere, rock-solid sentinel.

Graves Light is built upon the hazardous ledges of The Graves, a collection of rock outcroppings that appear appropriately named for the number of vessels that have met catastrophe on their jagged edges. However, The Graves was supposedly named in the 1600s for Thomas Graves, an English rear admiral who commanded a vessel in John Winthrop's fleet and was among the early Puritan settlers of Charlestown.

The outermost point of the Boston Harbor Islands national park area at a distance of eleven miles from Long Wharf, The Graves proved a menace to mariners in the centuries following the Puritans' arrival in Boston. An iron bell buoy was placed near the protruding rocks in the 1850s as a navigation aid. At the turn of the twentieth century, when a northern entrance to Boston Harbor was dredged to and from President Roads in order to accommodate deep-draft ships, a lighthouse was built at its entrance to warn of the dangerous ledges. When its lantern was first lit on September 1, 1905, Graves Light became the most powerful lighthouse along the New England coast.

Even after Graves Light's construction, there were still a number of shipwrecks in its vicinity, including the wreck of a latter-day

The heavy oak front doors to Graves Light are reached after scaling a forty-foot-ladder from the tower's base.

Graves Light guards the northern entrance to Boston Harbor.

Noah's Ark. In the midst of a dense fog on an April morning in 1938, the British freighter *City of Salisbury* was impaled on an unmarked reef, a half mile from The Graves. The ship carried some unusual cargo: a floating menagerie of jungle animals, including a dozen pythons, cobras, tropical birds, three hundred monkeys, and three small honey bears. Fortunately, all passengers (human and otherwise) were rescued before the *City of Salisbury* broke in half the following day. (See page 61 for information about diving near the wreck.)

While numerous boats have succumbed to the sea around The Graves, the lighthouse's mighty blocks of Cape Ann granite, seven feet thick at the base, are able to withstand the relentless punishment of the open ocean. The light from the 113-foot-tall beacon is visible for twenty-four nautical miles. The lantern, automated in 1976 and converted to solar power in 2001, emits two white flashes every twelve seconds.

Although the U.S. Coast Guard continues to operate and maintain the navigational beacon and fog signal, the lighthouse is privately owned. Since purchasing Graves Light and its outbuildings at auction in 2013 for nearly $1 million—the most ever paid for an American lighthouse at the time—David and Lynn Waller have done more than just slap a fresh coat of paint on this nautical fixer-upper, although the heavy oak front doors that are reached after scaling a forty-foot ladder from the tower's base have been painted bright regulation red. Using the original architectural drawings for Graves Light, the couple has meticulously replicated the lighthouse's origi-nal paneled ceilings, doors, handrails, and cabinets to build a new kitchen, library, master bathroom, bunk room, and service room.

In addition to cleaning and repairing Graves Light's exterior masonry, the Wallers have stabilized the old dock and added a shanty for storage. With plans to convert the lighthouse's original granite oil house to a guest cottage, the owners have added a second story as well as a replica copper roof and cupola to match the original. They are also rebuilding the 130 foot-catwalk connecting the tower to the oil house. It was swept away along with the fog signal house during the "Perfect Storm" of October 1991.

Graves Light is closed to the public, and private boats are prohibited from landing on The Graves without permission of the owners because of the danger posed by the rocks and surf. Graves Light is certainly in need of its share of sightseers, but cast your awe-inspired gaze from the water.

For more information, visit graveslightstation.com.

Boston Harbor Islands. *Photo Credits (Courtesy of Boston Harbor Island Alliance, Photographer Tom Kates) by Massachusetts Office of Travel & Tourism is licensed under CC BY-ND 2.0.*

Kayaking in Boston Harbor

The Wild Turkey Paddlers is an informal group that provides kayak enthusiasts with an opportunity to meet, participate in trips, and learn skills. As a member of the group, Jordan Jacobs has spent years paddling Boston Harbor and offers this advice.

"If you're paddling in the outer harbor, you need to be prepared for a full open-water experience. Always wear a personal flotation device, dress for the water temperature, and don't paddle alone. Each person should have all the requisite self- and assisted-rescue skills and have practiced dealing with a capsize safely. Leave a detailed float plan with an emergency contact that has the pertinent information about your launch point, planned route, and estimated time of return. Since you'll be sharing the waterways with motorboats, familiarize yourself with charts of the area, be mindful of the channels you cross, and make sure you're constantly visible.

"Gear should include a spare paddle and a boat with bulkheads and/or sufficient float bags to ensure a capsize doesn't sink your re-entry efforts. A VHF radio in a water-resistant pouch is a must if you're going in open water. While I never want anyone to depend on the Coast Guard or another craft for immediate assistance, if something unforeseen or dire occurs, you'd rather have substantial assistance on their way to you versus hoping someone happens upon you.

"I'd recommend boats a minimum of fourteen or fifteen feet in length that tend to have multiple bulkheads that trap buoyancy, which is essential in a capsize situation. The longer water line tends to facilitate a faster hull speed so those whose paddling skills are a little weak may be able to sustain a faster pace. Longer boats also have more of a sea kayak hull form versus a flatwater boat, and secondary stability for a boat in open water is a very desirable attribute!

"If you're heading out into open water, I'm a big proponent of working on your skills and stamina to deal with wind and current that aren't assisting you. Lots of trips start out smooth and happy and then become problematic when someone bonks or feels squirrely with deteriorating conditions. Some people hate being surfed; in open water we often have to take what comes along and don't have a choice. Having a minimum level of proficiency out there is not only essential to your personal and group safety, it will enable everyone to have more fun.

"Don't underestimate how dynamically the conditions can change out on Boston Harbor. In the morning it might be like glass, and on the way home you can be in two to three feet of textured water. Some people love it. Others will get pretty uneasy and scared, and scared people don't often respond well nor accept good advice when you need them to. Don't attempt a learning experience unless you have others who are far more experienced and can render the support that may be necessary on a day when you're specifically looking to expand your skills and experiences in the open water.

"I'm a big fan of checking conditions and utilizing them for a 'downhill' leg on the return trip. Some of the more interesting islands are around Boston Light and the Brewsters out to The Graves. Especially with some north winds, it gets quite lively. A great place to launch from is Malibu Beach near the gas tanks and the University of Massachusetts Boston off Morrissey Boulevard at the end of the off ramp on the right-hand side. It has great access at all tide levels and gives you great accessibility to the Spectacle Island and Long Island areas.

"Until everyone has their minimum proficiencies, though, it can be a gamble venturing out to the islands in Boston Harbor. I can't tell you how many times I've launched from Hull and gone through Hull Gut when it was dead flat and then found myself on the way home crossing from Boston Light in three- to four-foot swells trying to back through Hull Gut with apposing wind and tide flow. So for beginners still gaining their sea legs, I'd suggest paddling in Hingham Harbor and back into the Weir River. It's open but still removed from the Boston Harbor motorboat traffic.

"After having been paddling for many years, I've learned it's better to pass on a trip that is beyond the proficiency of a group than to just jump and hope for the best. No one should read about you because of a mishap out there."

The Wild Turkey Paddlers offers free skills sessions throughout the year. For more information, visit wtpaddlers.org.

Islands for
Landlubbers

The distinctive egg digesters of the Deer Island Wastewater Treatment Plant have become harbor landmarks.

Deer Island

THE TWELVE EGG-SHAPED STRUCTURES at the entrance to Boston Harbor often provoke a similar question among first-time visitors: "What the heck are those things?" Well, they are the 130-foot-tall sludge digesters of the massive Deer Island Wastewater Treatment Plant. These bulbous-bellied digesters do the dirty, but essential job of breaking down the sludge from wastewater sent to the plant by forty-three communities in metropolitan Boston. Capable of processing more than one billion gallons a day, the Deer Island plant sends treated wastewater nearly ten miles offshore through a concrete tunnel, twenty-four feet in diameter. Without these digesters—and the entire sewage treatment plant that opened in 2001—there wouldn't be a clean harbor, a revitalized waterfront, or even, possibly, a national park area.

Composting and portable toilets are available on the following islands: Deer, Nut, Lovells, Bumpkin, Grape.

The plant is the centerpiece of the $4.5 billion environmental restoration of Boston Harbor that marks the first time Bostonians can point to Deer Island with pride, rather than shame. For centuries, Deer Island was the dismal home of interned Native Americans, quarantined immigrants, orphans, paupers, and criminals. Even today, the voices of those who suffered there seem to whisper in the wind.

Now owned by the Massachusetts Water Resources Authority (MWRA), Deer Island was a different place when English settlers first arrived in the 1630s. Deer were known to escape wolves by swimming across the narrow Shirley Gut that once separated the island from the mainland. (Since the 1930s, when Shirley Gut was filled with sand, Deer Island has been a peninsula connected to the mainland at Winthrop.) The island was heavily wooded, dotted with freshwater ponds, and surrounded by tall bluffs on three sides. As the settlers harvested the island's timber to build their colony, this natural beauty was quickly transformed. Forty years later it would be shattered entirely.

Just over a half century after the Pilgrims sat down to the first Thanksgiving with the Wampanoag and their great sachem Massasoit in 1621, an uneasy peace between the encroaching colonists and Native Americans gave way to a bloody war. Led by Massasoit's son, Metacom, who was known to the English as "King Philip," Native Americans battled the colonists in King

Deer Island offers more than sixty acres of parkland with five miles of public trails.

Philip's War, which raged across New England from New Hampshire to Connecticut in 1675 and 1676. By the time the fighting was done, thousands were dead, colonial villages lay in ruins, and Native American populations were devastated. In proportion to the population of the time, King Philip's War was the deadliest conflict ever fought on American soil.

One of the saddest chapters in this brutal tale occurred on the shores of Deer Island. It was to this island that the Massachusetts Bay Colony forcibly interned hundreds of Native Americans, known as "Praying Indians." Though they had converted to Christianity and pledged their loyalty to the English, the settlers feared the Praying Indians, many of them from the Nipmuc Tribe, would join in arms with the enemy. That fear quickly evolved into paranoia and bigotry, and during the middle of the night on October 30, 1675, the English hurried them from Natick and other "praying towns" around Boston onto boats along the Charles River in Watertown, ferrying them to Deer Island.

Some historical accounts place the number of prisoners at five hundred, but Native American oral traditions put the total much higher. Whatever the number, the Native Americans suffered great hardships during the particularly harsh winter of 1675 and 1676. They were given few provisions and subsisted on clams and other shellfish. They lacked adequate shelter from the bitter cold but were not allowed to cut firewood. Colonial settlers were authorized to kill any Native American found off Deer Island not accompanied by an English guard. John Eliot (the minister who had converted the Native Americans) and Daniel Gookin visited in December 1675 and reported, "the island was bleak and cold, their wigwams poor and mean, their clothes few and thin."

Before the prisoners were released in May 1676, it is estimated that as many as half of them died from starvation or exposure. Many who survived were sold into slavery in the West Indies. Without question, it was one of the darkest moments in Boston's history, and one that continues to cast shadows on Deer Island.

Little improved on Deer Island. In the late 1840s, refugees fleeing Ireland's Great Hunger after the failure of the potato crop sold all they had for a one-way ticket to America and an opportunity to finally be free of the disease and death that savaged their homeland. In 1847 alone, nearly twenty-five thousand Irish citizens immigrated to Boston. By 1850, a third of the city's population was Irish.

So many refugees perished during the six-to-eight-week transatlantic voyage that the vessels carrying them became known as "coffin ships." But the situation was equally desperate for those who survived the journey, arriving in Boston without money, their health, or a place to live. Many refugees took up residence in the poor, unsanitary neighborhoods near the waterfront, such as the North End. The utterly destitute camped outdoors on Boston Common. Boston was overwhelmed, and many in Puritan Boston saw the sudden influx of the Irish as a threat to the city's economy, health, and way of life.

By the summer of 1847—the infamous "Black '47"—the quarantine station at Rainsford Island was no longer equipped to care for their sheer numbers. The city took possession of Deer Island for "sanitary purposes" and designated it as the new quarantine station. A hospital and associated buildings were built on the island's southern tip. Sick immigrants arriving in Boston were quarantined, though those who passed the initial inspection faced the prospect of being sent back to Deer Island if they became ill. Nearly five thousand refugees were quarantined on the island between 1847 and 1850, and approximately 850 died of diseases such as dysentery, typhus, and consumption. They were buried in unmarked graves, an ocean away from the home they were forced to flee and on the doorstep of the city that held the promise of a new life. Many of them were children, such as one-year-old Mary Connell, the first Irish refugee to die on Deer Island.

As Boston continued to grow during the second half of the nineteenth century, residential areas began to spring up around some of the city's less palatable social institutions, such as its homes for the poor and juvenile offenders. As a result, the city relocated these "undesirable elements" to Deer Island. In addition to the quarantine station, which was moved to Gallops Island in 1860, Deer Island became home to the city's almshouse, house of industry, schools for paupers, and houses of reformation. By the 1880s, the island was a veritable Atlantic Alcatraz, this time for city criminals. And in 1904, the Hill Prison, one of the first institutions in the United States built specifically for women, opened its doors. That building later became the Suffolk County House of Correction and remained on the island until 1991.

Like so many other islands in the harbor, Deer Island provided military protection for Boston. The island played a minor role in the Revolutionary War, when, in June 1775, a small band of patriots raided the island and seized eight hundred sheep and lambs, a few heads of cattle, and a handful of British prisoners. In May 1776, a naval battle took place in Shirley Gut between the American privateer *Franklin,* commanded by Captain James Mugford, and the British fleet—still lingering in the harbor.

At the onset of World War II, Fort Dawes was built on the southern tip of Deer Island to monitor the harbor entrance. The fort was named in honor of Revolutionary War hero William Dawes, who along with Paul Revere made a midnight ride to alert towns around Boston of the impending arrival of British troops in advance of the Battles of Lexington and Concord. The U.S. Navy used the fort to operate a radar and signal station, and naval guns on the island were capable of reaching targets as far north as Gloucester and as far south as Plymouth. Later in the war, Fort Dawes controlled the electronically operated minefields in the north channel of Boston Harbor, and nets were stretched from Deer Island to Hull to prevent submarines and German U-boats from entering Boston Harbor.

With the exception of the 1890s steam-driven pumping station that was restored as an MWRA visitor center, all of the island's military and

The Deer Island Pumping Station, built in 1895 and expanded in 1909, has since been restored as a visitor center. *Courtesy of the Library of Congress.*

institutional structures are long gone, as the island's landscape was drastically altered to make way for the current plant. (To shield Winthrop residents from construction, the island's drumlin was even moved to its northern side.)

The wastewater treatment plant occupies two-thirds of the island, but Deer Island offers more than sixty acres of parkland with five miles of public trails. A paved 2.6-mile walkway along the water, which is handicap accessible and stroller-friendly, and a more challenging hillside trail provide views of the ocean, the islands, and the city five miles away. Fishing is permitted in designated areas, and surf-casting is allowed from the gravel beach on the island's western shore. Deer Island is a popular spot with cyclists, joggers, and walkers, so the twenty-four-space parking lot is often filled on pleasant days in all seasons.

The north side of the island offers a fantastic overlook of the Boston skyline, and from the top of the 135-foot hill, children of all ages will delight in following the planes coming in for landing at Logan Airport. To the east of the overlook, near the water tower, is a simple granite bench on which "Rest Haven" is engraved. The bench honors the estimated 4,252 people buried on the island between 1847 and 1908—from the Irish immigrants who died at the quarantine station to the paupers and criminals unclaimed by relatives

VIEW OF THE NEW ALMS HOUSE for the CITY OF BOSTON in the STATE OF MASSACHUSETTS, ERECTING on DEER ISLAND in BOSTON HARBOR.
1849.
JOHN P. BIGELOW, MAYOR.
DESIGNED BY LUTHT, UWINJCY & GRIDLEY J P BRYANT
E J F BRYANT ARCHITECT

The almshouse, circa 1849. *Courtesy of the Library of Congress.*

Unveiled in 2019, a memorial to Irish immigrants who died on Deer Island stands in the shadows of the city skyline.

A memorial on Deer Island honors Judge A. David Mazzone, who ordered the cleanup of Boston Harbor.

or friends. The cemetery was moved to this side of the island after the U.S. Army bought it.

From the southern tip of Deer Island tankers and cargo ships from around the world pass Deer Island Light, an LED-powered beacon atop a steel skeletal frame that marks the dangerous shoals at the northern edge of President Roads along the harbor's main shipping channel. The present lighthouse stands near the brown cylindrical base that had supported two previous incarnations of Deer Island Light between 1890 and 2016.

A decades-long effort to commemorate the 850 Irish refugees buried in mass graves on Deer Island between 1847 and 1850 finally came to fruition in 2019 with the dedication of a sixteen-foot-tall granite Celtic cross on a bluff looking westward to

· PHILLIP alias METACOMET of Pokanoket.
Engraved from the original as Published by Church.

A copy of Paul Revere's engraving of Metacomet, published in *The Entertaining History of King Philip's War* by Thomas Church, Newport, 1772. *Courtesy of the Library of Congress.*

the city that the immigrants came so achingly close to reaching. The Irish exiles who survived their journey to Boston would transform the city, and an inscription on the memorial's base proclaims, "From dreams of a better life to the shores of our destiny was worth the sacrifice for those that follow."

Set against the backdrop of the revitalized harbor on Deer Island's northwest corner, a memorial bearing the inscription "the law secures to the people the right to a clean harbor" honors the late federal district court judge A. David Mazzone, whose landmark ruling led to the cleanup of Boston Harbor. No doubt Mazzone would be proud of how the new treatment plant has transformed Boston for the better and how his push toward progress provided Deer Island with a shining moment of redemption in a history that was tortured for far too long.

Michael Creasey, National Park Service

Michael Creasey has been the general superintendent of the National Parks of Boston, which includes the Boston Harbor Islands national park area, since 2015. Having worked at a range of National Park Service properties in the Northeast, he offers his unique perspective about what makes this park area so distinctive and shares his favorite places among the islands.

"The National Park Service and the city of Boston are lucky to have this urban interface where you have island landscapes that offer incredible experiences so nearby to more than one million people in the surrounding area. The general nature of how the park is organized is also unique. Islands are expensive to operate, and they are challenging because of the elements. These large landscapes can't be operated by just one entity. The Boston Harbor Islands Partnership doesn't place the National Park Service in the lead role of management. Our role is more of a facilitator. In the spirit of the partnership, we continue to facilitate a conversation about how we can make a collective impact to provide public access for recreational enjoyment and an opportunity for understanding what these places are about. I don't think any one agency can solve the problems, but together we can.

"Boston Light holds a special place in my soul. Boston Light is the icon that represents the national park area. I love coming into Boston Harbor and seeing it. It has such amazing history—how it was built, burned down, and then rebuilt. There's a real fascination with Boston Light being a gateway into Boston Harbor.

"I also love the diversity of Peddocks Island. What makes Peddocks special is its blend of the natural and cultural worlds. I enjoy the journey through the islands out to Peddocks, which is a little further from Long Wharf, and then arriving at the dock to be greeted by a landscape that evokes curiosity and exploration. I love the layered history of Fort Andrews and taking that walk along the beaches of Portuguese Bay into the living landscape of the cottages, which have a whole story in their own right. Then walking past the cottages to the natural world of West Head, the canopy of trees almost makes you feel as if you are walking in the South underneath live oaks."

ADDITIONAL INFORMATION

 Public guided tours of the Deer Island Wastewater Treatment Plant, operated by the Massachusetts Water Resources Authority (MWRA), are given on Tuesdays and Fridays of each month between April and November. Tours require reservations and begin at 9:30 a.m. Call ahead of time at (617) 660-7607. There is no admittance to the fenced-off treatment facility without prior approval. For more information, visit mwra.state.ma.us.

 Dogs permitted on leash.

Directions: Deer Island is located at the southern end of Tafts Avenue in Winthrop. The GPS address is 190 Tafts Avenue, Winthrop, MA 02152.

Snake Island

SNAKE ISLAND, NEAR DEER ISLAND and just a few hundred yards from the Winthrop mainland and Logan Airport, earned its name from its serpentine shape. Today, the island is owned by the town of Winthrop, and Snake Island has one of the largest remaining salt marshes in the Boston Harbor Islands. The mudflats and grassy clearings offer excellent offshore birding opportunities. In the late 1800s and early 1900s, lobstermen, clammers, and their families lived on the island seasonally. Today, licensed clammers harvest the productive mudflats between January and May. Access to Snake Island is easiest at high tide but may be restricted during the spring and summer to protect migrating shorebirds and the nesting grounds of American oystercatchers.

A view of Snake Island from the Winthrop shoreline.

Pathways diverge at World's End.

World's End

BOUNDED BY THE WEIR RIVER ON THE EAST and Hingham Harbor and its islands on the west, World's End occupies the tip of Cushing's Neck in the tony Boston suburb of Hingham. The drive down Martin's Lane to the reservation gives visitors just a taste of the lush scenery they will find inside the park, where a looping network of shady carriage paths evokes the grandeur of a seaside manor. This 251-acre reservation, one of the Boston Harbor "mainland" Islands, is graced with varied terrains of sandy coves, woodlands, fresh and saltwater marshes, grassy meadows, and granite cliffs. No one is quite sure how World's End earned its apocalyptic moniker, particularly given its bucolic setting that makes it the perfect place to spend an afternoon, following the road wherever it may lead.

Until early European settlers built a causeway to connect it to the mainland, World's End proper—which occupies just a portion of the total reservation—became an island at high tide. From overhead, the shape of the reservation, with the sandy causeway connecting the double drumlins of World's End to two mainland drumlins, is very similar to Spectacle Island.

Olmsted's layout for Brewer's property called for a network of curvilinear roads lined by tall, stately trees. *Nicole L. Vecchiotti.*

As on Spectacle Island, it is thought that Native Americans used World's End as a seasonal campsite. Native Americans set fish weirs and dug for shellfish on the island's shores. After European settlers arrived, Hingham farmers put the land to use for over three hundred years. No large-scale development ever occurred at World's End, though it certainly could have.

In 1855, John R. Brewer, a prominent Hingham resident, began acquiring parcels of land on Cushing's Neck, which he used to farm and raise livestock. By the 1880s, Brewer had acquired nearly all of the land that encompasses the present-day reservation, and his sprawling four-hundred-acre farm included the family's mansion along Martin's Lane, stables, homes for the farmhands, a sheepfold, a smokehouse, and even a house for the family's guinea pigs, which were exhibited at local fairs. It seems Brewer always had an interest in landscape design, planting ornamental trees on Cushing's Neck soon after he bought the property, and in 1886 this pastime led him to hire America's most famous landscape architect, Frederick Law Olmsted.

Olmsted had already achieved considerable fame for his work on New York's Central Park when he moved to Brookline, Massachusetts, in 1883. One cause for Olmsted's decision to relocate from New York to Brookline may have been his work on the twenty-year project we now know as Boston's Emerald Necklace, though it has been suggested as well that Olmsted was fond of Brookline because it embodied everything he believed a suburb should be. Though it might surprise some, given his success in having designed the nation's most celebrated public spaces, Olmsted was an early advocate of planned suburban communities that could combine the conveniences of cities with the charms of rural life. "No great town can long exist without great suburbs," he wrote in 1868.

Under Brewer's commission, Olmsted was hired to subdivide World's End into residential parcels. Although Brewer had no immediate intention of selling off these parcels, he wanted to be prepared in case he ran into financial difficulty. Olmsted's design for 163 subplots of varying sizes was Brewer's contingency plan.

Like many of the Boston Harbor Islands, World's End in the 1880s was relatively barren from centuries of agricultural use. It was Olmsted's pet interest in reforesting the islands that attracted him to Brewer's project. Olmsted desired to keep the pasture and meadow land open, so he didn't intend to plant groves of native trees that would eventually become a dense forest. Instead, his layout called for a network of curvilinear roads that hugged the natural contours of the drumlins and were lined by tall, stately trees such as English oaks, Norway maples, and American elms.

The Brewers built the cart paths and planted the tree seedlings fairly closely to Olmsted's original specifications. (The tree planting also extended to Sarah and Langlee Islands in Hingham Harbor, owned by the Brewer family at the time.) However, no subplot was ever sold, presumably because it wasn't a financial necessity. This partial execution of Olmsted's proposal has left the property with a system of roads that appear to lead nowhere, which can be charming and peculiar at the same time. After the Brewer family line died out in 1936, most of the property's buildings, including the mansion, were torn down and World's End fell into relative disuse.

It's hard to imagine, but this nearly realized subdivision was once under consideration as the potential home of the United Nations. In 1945, the newly created

Looking back to the Boston skyline from World's End.

international organization settled on the United States as the location for its headquarters, and metropolitan Boston and New York City were the two leading contenders. The United Nations' site committee ruled out any urban locations because of its sizable land requirements, and Massachusetts governor Maurice Tobin formed a committee to identify possible suburban locations for the world body. World's End was one of the sites on the initial list because of its availability of land and proximity to Boston, though it failed to make the final cut. (It certainly gives one pause to think of the United Nations headquartered in an area called World's End.)

However, other suburban Boston locations were still being considered when millionaire philanthropist John D. Rockefeller Jr. swooped in at the last minute and shocked everyone with a gift of six blocks of Manhattan real estate along the East River. Even though the committee from the start had eliminated all sites within ten miles of Manhattan, it reversed itself in a New York minute and accepted Rockefeller's gift, once again leaving Boston, its civic rival to the north, in the shadows of Gotham.

Twenty years after the United Nations flirtation, proposals were drawn to build a nuclear power plant on World's End, but it was eventually constructed in Plymouth. With the property under increasing threat of development, more than $450,000 was raised from public subscription to purchase it. In 1967, World's End was bought by the Trustees of Reservations—one of the oldest private land trusts in the world, conceived in 1891 by Olmsted's protégée and partner Charles Eliot.

Now that the seedlings have grown and saplings have matured, visitors to World's End can enjoy the fulfillment of the landscape that Olmsted designed more than a century ago. It's very easy for your eyes to remain focused on the rutted road ahead as it ascends and descends numerous hills and gracefully curves with the rolls of the land, but those who focus solely on the road ahead will miss out on spectacular water views, framed by the trees of which Olmsted was so fond. The 120-foot-high summit of Planter's Hill provides a stunning vista of the Boston skyline, Hingham Harbor, and Atlantic Ocean.

The Rocky Neck section of World's End lives up to its name and provides a much different feel from the broad, tree-lined carriage paths and open meadows found elsewhere in the reservation. With narrow trails that thread their way under a dense canopy of trees and along granite outcrops, Rocky Neck is much wilder and feels a little like the Maine coastline—with the black flies to match. What begins as a walk through the deep woods, where you wander through cobwebs and brush up against scrubby pine, ends with the meeting of land and water. Emerging onto the rocky precipices along the Weir River, you are confronted by the condominiums and homes along Nantasket Beach. Had Olmsted and Brewer's subdivision come to pass, it may have fit right in with these other residential developments. During the summer, the river is a popular anchoring spot for weekend boaters, and the chatter of sailors and the hum of jet-skis fill the air.

Recreational opportunities and a wide variety of educational programming for nature lovers and families make World's End a popular destination all year long. Even after a 2018 expansion, the reservation's parking lot can fill up quickly on weekends.

The restoration of tidal flow to a salt marsh dammed by settlers hundreds of years ago to grow hay has revived its ecosystem. It is a birder's paradise, providing habitats for grassland-nesting birds and is a great spot for viewing landbird migration, such as waterfowl, raptors, and herons. An elevated boardwalk leading to a bird blind along the salt marsh is a particularly good location for bird watching. Kayakers and fishermen can explore the miles of coastline along the reservation or venture to the islands in Hingham Harbor. The four miles of gravel carriageways and grassy trails are a natural draw for both walkers and joggers, while the benches scattered throughout the property and along the shore provide spots to rest and relax. In the winter, the snow-covered trails are popular with cross-country skiers.

Nicole L. Vecchiotti.

Frederick Law Olmsted's Reforestation Plan

In 1886, Frederick Law Olmsted described the Boston Harbor Islands, after centuries of deforestation, as "artificially bald, raw, bleak, prosaic, inhospitable." When the Pilgrims explored Boston Harbor in 1621, they found that Native Americans had cleared some of the islands from end to end to support their seasonal camps. After the Europeans settled in Boston, they further denuded the islands for their wood and transformed their landscapes to support farming and grazing.

Olmsted sought to restore the islands to their original vegetative state and argued that the attractiveness of Boston Harbor and its islands "reckoned no insignificant element of the trade and prosperity of the city." In addition, he reasoned that the lack of trees made the islands more susceptible to extreme weather conditions and contributed to their erosion into the sea.

"Once the islands were bodies of foliage. Seen one against another and grouping with wood headlands, they formed scenery of grace and amenity, cheerful, genial, hospitable. But long ago they were despoiled for petty private gains," Olmsted wrote in an 1886 article in *The Century*. "It would not lessen but enhance their values for these purposes to dress them again with the graces of naturally disposed foliage; and under a well-prepared system, patiently followed, it would cost little more every year to do this than is spent for an hour's exhibition of fireworks."

Olmsted submitted a formal report to the Boston Park Commissioners for the reforestation of the islands. Olmsted did not propose to turn the barren islands into landscaped "parks" similar to the Emerald Necklace, and no land was to be purchased. The plan was simply to plant native trees—such as pine, birch, and oak—on about four hundred acres at a cost of $5,000 a year for six years. The Park Commissioners, presumably more interested in investing civic money in pyrotechnic displays, rejected Olmsted's plan.

Although many of the harbor islands are again green with vegetation, the native habitats were never formally restored. Many of the islands' trees are invasive species or scrubby, pioneer species, such as staghorn sumac, that are among the first plants to return to an area that has been disturbed by activities such as agriculture and deforestation. Building on Olmsted's vision, park management is leading habitat restoration projects to eradicate invasive species and allow native vegetation to reclaim the islands.

The reservation is particularly exquisite in the fall when a vibrant palette emerges among Olmsted's trees. Walking through the wooded areas of Rocky Neck in autumn will bring to mind the opening stanza of Robert Frost's poem "The Road Not Taken":

> Two roads diverged in a yellow wood, / And sorry I could not travel both / And be one traveler, long I stood / And looked down one as far I could / To where it bent in the undergrowth . . .

The good news is that, unlike the traveler in Frost's poem, you don't have to fret about which road to take at World's End. If you have the time, you can travel them all.

ADDITIONAL INFORMATION

 Dogs permitted on leash.

 Mountain biking permitted on dirt roads.

Horseback riding permitted at a walking pace with purchase of an annual permit from The Trustees of Reservations.

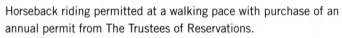 Summer solstice celebration in June, full moon hikes, and ecology programs for children and families. See Events section of The Trustees of Reservations website (thetrustees.org) or phone (781) 740-6665 for additional events.

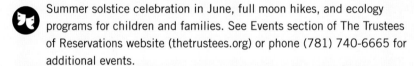 Secure moorings off the coast of World's End are available through the Hingham Harbormaster. Reservations and annual permit required. Call (781) 741-1450. For more information, visit hpd.org/198/Harbormaster.

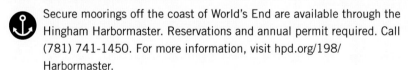 *Admission:* At the time of publication, open 8:00 a.m. to sunset year-round. Note parking lot is not plowed in winter. Admission is free for children and members of The Trustees of Reservations, $8 for nonmember adults on weekends and holidays, and $6 for nonmember adults on weekdays.

Directions: From Route 3, take exit 14 and follow Route 228 north toward Hingham for 6.5 miles. Turn left onto Route 3A and follow for 0.4 miles. Turn right onto Summer Street and, at the major intersection with Rockland Street, continue straight across onto Martin's Lane. Follow for 0.7 miles until it dead ends at the entrance.

Webb Memorial State Park

ON A SUMMER EVENING, THE PARKING LOT at Webb Memorial State Park is full, and walkers and joggers converge on the gravel paths snaking through the park. Fishermen unwind in chairs along the stony beach, waiting for the fish to bite, while picnickers spread their blankets alongside the carpet of yellow, white, and purple wildflowers filling the meadows. With such magnificent scenery, it's no wonder this recreation area is so popular with local North Weymouth residents.

Named in honor of William K. Webb, a former Weymouth police captain and World War II veteran, twenty-six-acre Webb Memorial State Park occupies a peninsula extending into Hingham Bay at the end of Weymouth Neck, flanked by the Fore River to the west and the Back River to the east. Until the area around George Lane Beach was filled in, the peninsula became an island at high tide when the Back River cut it off from the rest of Weymouth. Watching local residents and other visitors enjoying the tranquil park today, it's hard to imagine that as recently as the 1960s this piece of land was home to something much different—a noisy, smelly fertilizer plant.

Weymouth Neck was used as a seasonal campsite by Native Americans, and it was part of an area they called "Wessagussett," Algonquian for "by the small saltwater cove." Europeans principally used the land for agriculture until 1861, when the Bradley Fertilizer Company moved in and built a massive complex of buildings along the bank of the Back River. In addition to the factory, facilities included a blacksmith shop, furnaces, wharves, and grease extraction tanks. Indeed, the Bradley Fertilizer Company was quite an operation, capitalizing on the quintessentially American quest to maintain a green expanse of lawn—which isn't as modern a phenomenon as you might think. Bradley's advertisements, even back

A bench looking out on a cove at Webb Memorial State Park.

in the 1890s, admonished consumers that "a rusty, uneven faded out lawn is a disgrace to any true American."

It is somewhat ironic that something as lovely and refreshing as a green, grassy yard could be the end result of such a squalid production process. While the company boasted that its fertilizers combined the "quick action of Peruvian guano and the lasting properties of bone," the smell of the raw materials used in the production process—including bones, fish scraps, animal hides, and dried blood—earned the area around the plant the nickname of "Skunk Island." Worse than the smell, perhaps, were the hazardous consequences that came from the plant's large-scale mixing of chemicals, such as a fire in 1946 that melted the factory's acid tanks. The acid was so strong that it set the roads aflame and ate through the tires of two fire trucks responding to the scene, which had to be abandoned. Despite this, the fertilizer factory did not close until 1966.

Just as other Boston Harbor Islands have been used for military fortifications since the Puritans dropped anchor, Weymouth Neck played a role in protecting Boston from potential attacks as well—though this time it was

A meadow of wildflowers at Webb Memorial State Park.

during the Cold War. In 1954, the federal government purchased a site on the peninsula and built a Nike missile base.

During the Cold War era, the threat of foreign attacks on American soil shifted from the sea to the air. The nation's coastal defenses came to rely heavily on the Nike anti-aircraft missile system, which was not only the most expensive missile system ever deployed, but also the most widespread, with three hundred sites in thirty states. Sites were chosen to protect urban areas throughout the United States, bringing a little bit of *Dr. Strangelove* to suburbs such as Weymouth. The missiles, capable of carrying small nuclear warheads, were stored in underground silos and controlled by a radar system on what is now Spinnaker Island, across Hingham Bay.

The missile site (located on the west side of Webb Memorial State Park) was deactivated in the 1970s, and the property was transferred to the Commonwealth of Massachusetts, which converted it to parkland and officially opened Webb Memorial State Park in 1980.

However, the park was still plagued by a dreadful legacy of environmental contamination left behind by both the Bradley Fertilizer Company and the American Agricultural Chemical Co., which bought the site in 1900. Long before the idea of the park came to be, both companies buried industrial waste, such as iron oxide, lead sulfate sludge, coal ash, and animal bones.

ConocoPhillips, which acquired American Agricultural Chemical Co., spearheaded an extensive environmental cleanup of the park that took place between 2005 and 2008. Just as Spectacle Island has been transformed from its checkered past as a dumping ground to parkland, so too has Webb Memorial State Park been reborn as a recreational area for all to enjoy.

As with most of the Boston Harbor Islands, Webb Memorial State Park consists of drumlins formed by glaciers, although much of the original topography has been altered by grading and landscaping. Despite its small size, the park contains a wide variety of landscapes, such as meadows of wildflowers, groves of sumac and birch trees, and wetlands filled with cattails. During the spring, cherry blossoms burst forth with bright pink colors. Although swimming is not permitted, the beaches are good spots from which to launch your kayak to explore the islands in Hingham Bay. A 1.5-mile loop on the aptly named Robert B. Ambler Walkway, dedicated to the memory of a former state representative who was instrumental in the park's preservation, is a gentle walk.

Donald F. Haviland Memorial

One of the more moving monuments at Webb Memorial State Park honors Commander Donald F. Haviland of the United States Merchant Marine. When World War II broke out, Haviland was nearing the age of fifty and too old to re-enlist in the Marines. Undeterred, he volunteered for the Merchant Marine instead. The Merchant Marine's delivery of supplies provided a critical lifeline to the Allies during the war, and missions were so perilous that they suffered a higher proportion of casualties than any other service, except the Marines.

Born in Weymouth, Haviland served as chief engineer on the SS *Henry Bacon*, which transported war supplies and Norwegian war refugees between the Soviet Union and Great Britain in February 1945. A heavy gale in the Arctic Ocean forced the *Henry Bacon* to drop out of its forty-four-ship convoy. Alone and vulnerable off the Norwegian coast, it came under attack by German bombers and began to sink. The Norwegians and some crew, including Haviland, filled the lifeboats, but they simply couldn't accommodate the remaining personnel.

When this situation became known to Haviland, he insisted on giving his place to an eighteen-year-old messman from Revere, pleading with him, "Come on, kid, get into that damn lifeboat!" Shortly thereafter, he and fourteen other crew members went down with the ship. Haviland posthumously received the Merchant Marine's highest honor. He was also honored by the Soviet Union and Norway.

A plaque in the park tells Haviland's story, and the adjacent flagpole, which can be seen in the harbor areas around Weymouth Neck, proudly flies the colors of the United States. The water of the Back River is an appropriate backdrop for honoring this mariner and hero.

Donald F. Haviland Memorial at Webb Memorial State Park.

A granite block across the channel from Grape Island commemorates the Grape Island Alarm of May 1775 and salutes the Weymouth militiamen who "repulsed an attempt by the British to secure supplies from Grape Island for General Howe's beleaguered army in Boston." However, it's the smaller memorials to prominent Weymouth citizens and civic leaders spread throughout this well-loved recreation area that demonstrate its connection to the local residents. And as a visit to Webb Memorial State Park on a summer evening will attest, that connection is even stronger now that the park has been revitalized.

A monument to the Grape Island Alarm at Webb Memorial State Park.

ADDITIONAL INFORMATION

Dogs permitted on leash.

Directions: Take Route 3A to Weymouth; turn north on Neck Street, which changes name to River Street; and follow to the end. The GPS address is 371 River Street, Weymouth, MA 02191.

Nut Island

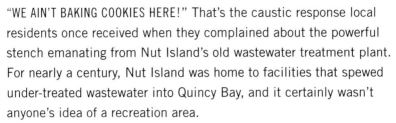

"WE AIN'T BAKING COOKIES HERE!" That's the caustic response local residents once received when they complained about the powerful stench emanating from Nut Island's old wastewater treatment plant. For nearly a century, Nut Island was home to facilities that spewed under-treated wastewater into Quincy Bay, and it certainly wasn't anyone's idea of a recreation area.

How times have changed! Thanks to the replacement of the wastewater treatment plant, a key component in the overall clean-up of Boston Harbor, Nut Island has been revitalized and is now a delightful place to visit. Anglers cast their lines off the long fishing pier. Paved paths along the shoreline provide walkers and joggers with pleasant views. And any smell in the air now is likely to be the fragrance of colorful wildflowers or the salty breeze coming off the harbor.

Nut Island, once separated from the mainland by a sandbar that disappeared at high tide, is now a twenty-acre peninsula firmly attached to the end of Houghs Neck, a tight-knit Quincy neighborhood whose bluffs provide fantastic views of the harbor and Boston skyline. In the late 1800s and early 1900s, Houghs Neck was a popular summer resort with lively social affairs drawing Bostonians and tourists from all around New England, and these vacationers often spent the day swimming and picnicking on nearby Nut Island, which according to legend gained its name from a nut tree that once grew there.

In the latter half of the nineteenth century this cavorting gave way to a spookier pastime. Nearly a half century after Donald McKay and others had given rise to a proud shipbuilding history across the harbor, Nut Island became a graveyard for a vast number of sailing vessels, including steamers and some of the U.S. Navy's most powerful and historic ships from the Civil War. Thomas Butler & Co., a marine junk company, purchased the ships, towed them

Nut Island abounds with wildflowers.

to Nut Island, and grounded them on the beach. Workers stripped them of their engines and other components; removed every piece of iron, brass, and copper; and sent the valuable material back to Boston for resale. Then, all that remained of these once-proud ships was set ablaze to salvage any remaining metal, with the devouring flames oftentimes illuminating the night sky, providing a spectacular sight for crowds that lined the hills and shores for miles around.

The first of the ships to meet their ignominious end at Nut Island was the steam frigate USS *Niagara* in the 1880s. The *Niagara*, the largest wooden ship in the world when it was launched in the 1850s, served in the Civil War and was one of the two vessels that laid the first transatlantic telegraph cable. Other warships that returned to the sea at Nut Island included the USS *Wyoming*, the USS *Brooklyn*, and the USS *Galena*, one of the first Civil War ironclads and a sister ship of the famous USS *Monitor*.

The *Brooklyn* gained its fame as part of the fleet under the command of Civil War hero David Farragut, whose statue stands watch over Pleasure Bay in South Boston. The *Brooklyn* saw action in heated Civil War battles, including the capture of both New Orleans and Mobile. During the Battle of Mobile Bay, the *Brooklyn* watched as the USS *Tecumseh* struck a tethered naval

A welcoming bench looks out on Quincy Bay and the Boston skyline.

mine (known at the time as a "torpedo"). Seeing this unfolding calamity, the *Brooklyn* wavered as it was about to enter the bay. This hesitation supposedly caused Farragut (who was reportedly lashed to the rigging of the USS *Hartford*) to give the order, "Damn the torpedoes! Full speed ahead!"

Some of the cottages on Houghs Neck were built with relics of these doomed warships and steamers. Pilot houses, cabin doors, windows, and other salvaged parts were incorporated into the cottages on Houghs Neck, making for a quirky architectural hodgepodge.

The Houghs Neck residents endured some noisy days during the 1870s when Nut Island was used to test some of the largest cannons ever seen at that time. These massive fifteen-inch guns were cast at the South Boston Iron Company foundry, which had been supplying ordnance to the military since the War of 1812. Colonel Norman Wiard, a well-known inventor of guns and projectiles who was frequently consulted by President Abraham Lincoln during the Civil War, conducted the gunnery experiments.

Wiard's monster cannons used the eroding bluffs of Princes Head on Peddocks Island for target practice. Hundreds of people, including American military officers and artillery experts, watched in awe as the booming cannons, weighing more than twenty tons, thundered with every test.

The guns hurtled five-hundred-pound shots, which—when successful—pierced the solid wrought-iron target plates on Princes Head about a mile across the water. However, these experiments didn't always go as planned. On one occasion, the ordnance sailed over the target and landed in a cemetery in Hull. The experiments cost nearly half a million dollars, and Wiard would later come under criticism for giving false reports of success and fleecing the government out of $250,000 by engaging in extravagant expenditures during his summers in Boston.

Today, these experiments are commemorated with a modest monument set against the backdrop of Princes

David Farragut, lashed to the rigging of the *Hartford*, orders the *Brooklyn* to "Damn the torpedoes!" *Courtesy of the Library of Congress.*

Once the largest wooden ship in the world, the USS *Niagara* met its fate on Nut Island. *Courtesy of the Library of Congress.*

Head, which still bears the scars from the target practices. The centerpiece of the monument is a small, rusted remnant of an 11-inch Rodman rifled cannon that burst during a test-firing. It is flanked by two projectiles used in that type of cannon.

Around the turn of the twentieth century, Nut Island became home to a sewage pump station. A wastewater treatment facility replaced it in 1952, but the plant's open concrete tanks and discharge into the bay long assaulted the eyes and noses of the "Neckers," residents of the Houghs Neck neighborhood.

A memorial to the cannon experiments that once took place on Nut Island with Princes Head in the background.

Ironically, bottom-feeding fish such as flounder—with apologies to The Standells, who coined the infamous lyrics—"loved that dirty water." They flourished in the warm water and sludge discharged by the old treatment plants and, somewhat dubiously, Houghs Neck became known as the "Flounder Capital of the World," attracting fishermen from as far away as South Carolina. Eventually, though, the fish—like the Neckers—had enough of the pollution.

As part of the massive Boston Harbor cleanup, a new headworks facility replaced Nut Island's offensive wastewater treatment plant in 1998. This headworks removes large objects as well as sand and gravel from sewage piped from twenty-one communities south and west of Boston. The screened wastewater is then pumped through a 4.8-mile tunnel under Boston Harbor to Deer Island for treatment.

Thanks in large part to the sustained activism of the Neckers, along with the opening of the headworks facility, Nut Island became a revitalized, landscaped park area in 1999. Silver vents dotting the park are reminders that sewage treatment operations continue at the island owned by the Massachusetts Water Resources Authority (MWRA), but the redbrick headworks building, with its sloping green roof, descends four stories underground and is eclipsed by the beauty of the surroundings.

The pier at Nut Island is a popular spot for fishing.

How Boston's Wastewater Treatment System Works

The $4.5 billion cleanup of Boston Harbor has been the catalyst for the revitalization of the Boston Harbor Islands. The new facilities, built and operated by the Massachusetts Water Resources Authority (MWRA), have reversed the deteriorating water quality and made Boston Harbor one of the cleanest in the United States. MWRA's wastewater facilities serve forty-three communities, nearly half of the population of Massachusetts, and the amount of sewage treated by the MWRA system is enough to fill the Prudential Tower three times each day.

But how exactly does the wastewater treatment process work? First, sewage is transported to headworks facilities, such as the one on Nut Island, where grit and large objects are removed. Pumps then send the wastewater to the treatment plant on Deer Island.

At Deer Island, preliminary treatment allows for the settling of mud and sand, which is taken to a landfill for environmentally safe disposal. Then, the wastewater flows to primary settling tanks where up to 60 percent of the solids settle as a mixture of sludge and water. After that, secondary treatment occurs; oxygen is added to speed the growth of microbes that will consume the waste before it settles to the bottom of secondary tanks. The remaining sludge is then processed in those gigantic, landmark egg digesters, which mimic our own digestion process (in fact, the temperature is maintained at ninety-eight degrees) to break the sludge down into methane gas, carbon dioxide, solid organic byproducts, and water. The two geodesic dome tanks at Deer Island store the methane, which is used to help power the plant.

The remaining sludge—which is 94 percent water—is pumped back under the harbor to the Fore River pelletizing facility in Quincy through a fourteen-inch pipe. There it is dewatered, heat-dried, and converted into fertilizer pellets, which can be applied to crops, lawns, and gardens. The remaining wastewater is disinfected, and the effluent is discharged east of Deer Island into Massachusetts Bay by means of a 9.5-mile outfall tunnel more than 250 feet below the ocean floor. Toward the end of the tunnel, more than fifty release points allow the dilution of the effluent in deeper waters off the coast.

Although it's small and parking is limited, Nut Island offers plenty of opportunities to enjoy the harbor. Trails lead to views of other harbor islands, as well as Quincy Bay to the west and Hingham Bay to the east. Evening is a particularly pleasant time to visit. As the sun sets near the Boston skyline, fishermen cast their lines in hopes of nabbing some of the rebounding populations of striped bass, squid, mackerel, and bluefish. And, yes, the flounder have returned as well.

During the summer, dragonflies and butterflies dance amid a golden blanket of wildflowers that runs to the edge of the (now) blue sea. There are over twenty species of wildflowers at Nut Island, including Queen Anne's lace, lupine, coreopsis, dianthus, castilleja, and gaillardia. Wild roses, day lilies, and buttercups also provide pockets of color throughout the park. It's true that you still may not smell cookies at Nut Island, but you can certainly stop and smell the flowers.

ADDITIONAL INFORMATION

Dogs permitted on leash.

Directions: Take Route 3A to Quincy and turn north on Sea Street. Follow the road, which changes names to Sea Avenue, to the end and turn right at the entrance to the park.

Harbor & Island Resources

shunyufan/Getty Images

Get Involved!

BOSTON HARBOR NOW

When the Boston Harbor Islands became a unit of the National Park System in 1996, the new national park area was established with a unique public-private model for park development and funding. While the National Park Service plays a facilitating role, a partnership of federal, state, city, and nonprofit agencies governs the national park area as a whole.

Among the eleven members of the Boston Harbor Islands Partnership is the nonprofit Boston Harbor Now, which supports the park's activities through fundraising, programming, planning, and oversight. It promotes the use and awareness of the national park area and helps steward development on the harbor islands and forty-three-mile Boston Harborwalk trail that runs along the waterfront. Created in 2016 after the merger of the Boston Harbor Island Alliance and the Boston Harbor Association, Boston Harbor Now raises and manages the public and private resources to support the park, invests in park facilities, and partners with waterfront communities to prepare for rising sea levels. The nonprofit is involved in the procurement and management of vendors, business development, and marketing of the park. Plus, it coordinates free public programming, such as Sunday jazz concerts on Spectacle Island and living history programs on Georges Island.

Boston Harbor Now also hosts community cruises of Boston Harbor, coordinates free access to the islands for thousands of underserved Boston-area youth annually, and provides free ferry days to Spectacle and Georges Islands several times a year. (Save the Harbor/Save the Bay also provides free ferry cruises to the islands.) Much goes on behind the scenes, too. The organization coordinates fundraising efforts, lobbies on behalf of the park, and supports educational programming.

For more information on Boston Harbor Now, visit bostonharbornow.org.

FRIENDS OF THE BOSTON HARBOR ISLANDS

The blue-shirted members of the Friends of the Boston Harbor Islands are welcome beacons guiding the way for visitors to the national park area. The volunteers are common sights on any island excursion, giving tours and providing visitor services at the Boston Harbor Islands Welcome Center on the Rose Kennedy Greenway, on Spectacle Island, and at the Georges Island information booth. The Friends also advocate for the islands' preservation and organize boat trips, such as their annual New Year's Day island cruise that has become a Boston Harbor tradition. The organization's community outreach volunteers create exhibits and displays, give talks, and distribute free books about the harbor islands to libraries in the metropolitan Boston area.

The Friends evolved from the efforts of the Boston Harbor Islands Volunteer Corps, organized in 1979 by Suzanne Gall Marsh. Nearly twenty years before the creation of the national park area and the cleanup of Boston Harbor, the Friends were the early champions of the harbor islands. They pioneered boat trips to otherwise inaccessible islands, such as Calf and Rainsford Islands. Some members commit hundreds of volunteer hours each year, simply out of their love of the islands, and there are Friends who've been with the organization since its inception. "It's uplifting to realize the longevity of the volunteers who are involved," says Suzanne Gall Marsh. "There are people who have been involved for more than twenty-five years and have gotten their family members involved. Volunteers sharpen their skills and develop new ones.

"The Friends have been a very positive force in people's lives, and people have become personal friends. I'm so proud to be part of a group of people who love the islands and have done such good things for them."

To join the Friends of the Boston Harbor Islands, visit fbhi.org.

VOLUNTEERING

The National Park Service coordinates the volunteer services of many partners, such as the U.S. Coast Guard Auxiliary, Friends of the Boston Harbor Islands, and corporate and community groups. The park offers many volunteer opportunities including a variety of citizen science projects, which provides hands-on opportunities for members of the community to connect with nature while contributing to scientific research. The park sponsors year-round Stewardship Saturdays during which volunteers work alongside park staff to clear invasive species, protect habitat areas, and improve trails. Volunteers can also assist at special events and at island visitor centers.

For more information, visit bostonharborislands.org.

Resources

BOSTON HARBOR TRANSPORTATION

Boston Harbor Islands Ferry
1 Long Wharf
Boston, MA 02110
(617) 223-8666
bostonharborislands.org

Boston Harbor Water Taxi
1 Long Wharf
Boston, MA 02110
(617) 227-4320
bostonharborcruises.com/water-taxi

MBTA Harbor Express
Boston, MA
(617) 222-3200
mbta.com/schedules_and_maps
/boats

Rowes Wharf Water Transport
60 Rowes Wharf
Boston, MA 02110
(617) 406-8584 (reservations,
water taxi pickup)
roweswharfwatertransport.com

Winthrop Ferry
707 Shirley St.
Winthrop, MA 02152
(617) 846-1705 x3
town.winthrop.ma.us/ferry

CRUISES AND CHARTERS

Boston Belle Charters
333 Victory Rd.
Quincy, MA 02171
(617) 932-5533
bostonbellecharters.com

Boston Green Cruises
60 Rowes Wharf
Boston, MA 02110
(617) 261-6620
bostongreencruises.com

Boston Harbor Cruises
1 Long Wharf
Boston, MA 02110
(617) 227-4321
(877) 733-9425 (toll free)
bostonharborcruises.com

Boston Island Charters
Captain John Dinga
(617) 645-0971
bostonislandscharters.com

Charles Riverboat Company
100 CambridgeSide Place
Cambridge, MA 02141
(617) 621-3001
charlesriverboat.com

Classic Harbor Line
60 Rowes Wharf
Boston, MA 02110
(617) 951-2460
boston-sailing.com

Classic Sail Boston
(844) 724-5267
classicsailboston.com

Harbor Island Charters
123 Main St.
Hull, MA 02045
(781) 925-2404
harborislandcharters.com

Liberty Boston
67 Long Wharf
Boston, MA 02110
(617) 742-0333
libertyfleet.com

Massachusetts Bay Lines
60 Rowes Wharf
Boston, MA 02110
(617) 542-8000
massbaylines.com

Odyssey Cruises
60 Rowes Wharf
Boston, MA 02110
(866) 307-2469
odysseycruises.com

Rowes Wharf Water Transport
60 Rowes Wharf
Boston, MA 02110

(617) 406-8584 (reservations,
captain)
(617) 261-6620 (office, charters,
groups)
roweswharfwatertransport.com

Spirit of Boston
Commonwealth Pier
200 Seaport Blvd.
Boston, MA 02210
(866) 310-2469
spiritcruises.com

RECREATION

Boaters' Resources

MarineMax Russo Boston
24-R Ericsson St.
Boston, MA 02122
(617) 288-1000
marinemax.com

MarineMax Russo Hingham
335 Lincoln St.
Hingham, MA 02043
(781) 785-3619
marinemax.com

Diving

Boston SCUBA
256 Marginal St.
East Boston, MA 02128
(617) 418-5555
bostondiving.com
» *Certification & Diving Excursions*

East Coast Divers
213 Boylston St.
Brookline, MA 02445
(617) 277-2216
ecdivers.com
» *Certification & Diving Excursions*

Mass Diving
247 West Central St.
Natick, MA 01760
(508) 651-0698
massdiving.com
» *Certification & Diving Excursions*

South Shore Divers
99 Bridge St.
Weymouth, MA 02191
(781) 331-1144
southshoredivers.com
» *Certification & Equipment Rental*

Fishing Charters

AnglerFish Guides
333 Victory Rd.
Quincy, MA 02171
(781) 285-8862
anglerfishguides.com

Boston Fishing Charters
Bay Pointe Marina
64 Washington Court
Quincy, MA 02169
(781) 400-0400
bostonfishingcharters.com

Boston Fishstix
Marina Bay

Quincy, MA 02171
(617) 233-6090
bostonfishstix.com

Boston Fish Tales
98 Crystal Ave.
Revere, MA 02151
(617) 549-2439
bostonfishtales.com

Boston Harbor Charters
Town River Marina
674 Southern Artery
Quincy, MA 02169
(508) 326-9287

Boston Sportfishing
Mederios Dock
696 East 1st St.
South Boston, MA 02127
(617) 775-7745 (land line)
(617) 365-8610 (cell)
bostonsportfishing.com

City Slicker Charters
Crystal Cove Marina
529 Shirley St.
Winthrop, MA 02152
(781) 641-3474
bostonboat.com

C.J. Victoria Fishing Charters
Winthrop Town Pier
707 Shirley St.
Winthrop, MA 02152
(617) 283-5801
cjvictoria.com

First Bite Charters
Houghs Neck Maritime Center
137 Bay View Ave.
Quincy, MA 02169
(617) 438-9103
firstbitecharters.com

Fishing Frenzy Charters
28 Constitution Rd.
Charlestown, MA 02129
(617) 275-6670
bostonfishingfrenzy.com

Light 'n Fly Fishing Charters
Hull, MA 02045
(727) 480-1257
lightnfly.com

Lucky 7 Fishing Charters
(781) 710-1190
fishlucky7.com

Midnight Charter
83 Merryknoll Rd.
Weymouth, MA 02191
(617) 653-3772
charterfishboston.com

Reel Dream Charters
Marina Bay
333 Victory Rd.
Quincy, MA 02171
(617) 909-7122
reeldreamcharters.com

Sawdust Sportfishing
Hingham Shipyard Marinas

24 Shipyard Dr.
Hingham, MA 02043
(508) 274-7072
sawdustsportfishing.com

Kayak, Canoe, Sailboat, and Rowboat Rentals/Lessons

Billington Sea Kayak
41 Branch Point Rd.
Plymouth, MA 02360
(508) 746-5644
billingtonseakayak.com
» *Kayaking & Canoeing—Rentals & Lessons*

Black Rock Sailing School
Charlestown Marina
8 13th St.
Charlestown, MA 02129
(617) 639-3061
blackrocksailingschool.com
» *Sailing—Lessons*

Boston Harbor Boat Rentals
70 East India Row
Boston, MA 02110
(617) 240-2900
bostonharborboatrentals.com
» *Sailing—Rentals*

Boston Harbor Sailing Club
Rowes Wharf
Boston, MA 02110
(617) 720-0049
bostonharborsailing.com
» *Sailing—Rentals & Lessons*

Boston Rowing Center
88 Sleeper St.
Boston, MA 02210
(781) 925-5433
bostonrowingcenter.org
» *Rowing—Lessons*

Boston Sailing Center
54 Lewis Wharf
Boston, MA 02110
(617) 227-4198
bostonsailingcenter.com
» *Sailing—Rentals & Lessons*

Charles River Canoe & Kayak
15 Broad Canal Way
Cambridge, MA 02142
(617) 965-5110
paddleboston.com
» *Paddle boarding, Kayaking & Canoeing—Rentals, Lessons & Guided Tours*

Community Boating, Inc.
21 David Mugar Way
Boston, MA 02114
(617) 523-1038
community-boating.org
» *Sailing, Paddle boarding & Kayaking—Rentals & Lessons*

Courageous Sailing Center
Charlestown Navy Yard
Pier 4
Boston, MA 02129
(617) 242-3821
courageoussailing.org
» *Sailing—Rentals & Lessons*

Hingham Bay Racing
P.O. Box 540
Hingham, MA 02043
hinghambayracing.org
» *Sailing—Races*

Hingham Maritime Center
32 Summer St.
Hingham, MA 02043
(781) 741-5225
hinghammaritime.org
» *Sailing & Rowing—Lessons*

The Nahant Dory Club
Tudor Wharf
Nahant, MA 01908
doryclub.org
» *Sailing—Lessons & Racing*

Nantasket Kayaks
48 George Washington Blvd.
Hull, MA 02045
(781) 962-4899
nantasketkayaks.com
» *Kayaking & Paddle boarding— Rentals & Guided Tours*

Piers Park Sailing
95 Marginal St.
East Boston, MA 02128
(617) 561-6677
piersparksailing.org
» *Sailing—Lessons & Adaptive Sailing Program*

SailTime
Fan Pier
1 Marina Park Dr.

Boston, MA 02210
(617) 899-6815
sailtime.com
» *Sailing—Rentals & Charters*

U.S. Coast Guard Auxiliary
nws.cgaux.org
» *Boating—Courses*

United States Power Squadrons
(888) 367-8777
usps.org
» *Boating—Courses*

Wild Turkey Paddlers
wtpaddlers.org
» *Informational Kayaking Group—*
Skill Sessions & Outings

Marinas

Bare Cove Marina
3 Otis St.
Hingham, MA 02043
(781) 733-0068
barecovemarina.com

Boston Bay Marina
84 Condor St.
East Boston, MA 02128
(617) 569-5212
bostonbaymarina.com

Boston Harbor Shipyard & Marina
256 Marginal St.
East Boston, MA 02128
(617) 561-1400
bhsmarina.com

Boston Waterboat Marina
66 Long Wharf (North Side)
Boston, MA 02110
(617) 523-1027
bostonwaterboatmarina.com

Boston Yacht Haven
87 Commercial Wharf
Boston, MA 02110
(617) 367-5050
thebostonyachthaven.com

Captain's Cove Marina
1 Cove Way
Quincy, MA 02169
(617) 328-3331
captainscovemarina.com

Captain Jack's Viking Marina
554 Pleasant St.
Winthrop, MA 02152
(617) 539-4406
captainjacksmarina.com

Charlestown Marina
1 Pier 8, 13th St.
Charlestown, MA 02129
(617) 242-2020
charlestownmarina.com

Cohasset Harbor Marina
33 Parker Ave.
Cohasset, MA 02025
(781) 337-1964
cohassetharbormarina.com

Constitution Marina
28 Constitution Rd.
Boston, MA 02129
(617) 241-9640
constitutionmarina.com

Crystal Cove Marina
529 Shirley St.
Winthrop, MA 02152
(617) 846-7245
crystalcovemarina.com

Fan Pier Marina
1 Marina Park Dr.
Boston, MA 02210
(617) 443-9200
fanpiermarina.com

Hingham Harbor Marina
26 Summer St.
Hingham, MA 02043
(781) 749-0076
hinghamharbormarina.com

Hingham Shipyard Marinas
24 Shipyard Dr.
Hingham, MA 02043
(781) 749-2222
hinghamshipyardmarinas.com

Marina at Admirals Hill
305 Commandants Way
Chelsea, MA 02150
(617) 889-4002
mybostonmarina.com

The Marina at Rowes Wharf
50 Rowes Wharf

Boston, MA 02110
(617) 748-5013
themarinaatroweswharf.com

Marina Bay Boston
333 Victory Rd.
Quincy, MA 02171
(617) 847-1800
marinabayboston.com

MarineMax Boston
Bay Pointe Marina
64 Washington Court
Quincy, MA 02169
(617) 471-1777
marinemax.com

Seaport Landing Marina
154 Lynnway
Lynn, MA 01902
(781) 592-5821
ci.lynn.ma.us

Steamboat Wharf Marina
48 George Washington Blvd.
Hull, MA 02045
(781) 925-0044
steamboatwharfmarina.com

Sunset Bay Marina
2 A St.
Hull, MA 02045
(781) 925-2828
sunsetbayhull.com

Tern Harbor Marina
275 River St.
Weymouth, MA 02191

(781) 337-1964
ternharbormarina.com

Town River Marina
674 Southern Artery
Quincy, MA 02169
(617) 745-9813
townriver.com

Wessagussett Yacht Club
212 Wessagussett Rd.
North Weymouth, MA 02191
(781) 335-9800
wyc-online.org

Yacht Clubs

Boston Harbor Yacht Club
1805 Day Blvd.
South Boston, MA 02127
(617) 269-5641
bostonharboryc.com

Columbia Yacht Club
1825 Day Blvd.
South Boston, MA 02127
(617) 269-9831
columbiayc.us

Cottage Park Yacht Club
76 Orlando Ave.
Winthrop, MA 02152
(617) 846-2792
cpyc.org

Dorchester Yacht Club
100 Playstead Rd.
Dorchester, MA 02125

(617) 436-1002
dorchesteryachtclub.com

East Boston Yacht Club
1 Rice St.
East Boston, MA 02128
(617) 567-9698
eastbostonyachtclub.com

Hingham Yacht Club
211 Downer Ave.
Hingham, MA 02043
(781) 749-9779
hinghamyachtclub.com

Hull Yacht Club
5 Fitzpatrick Way
Hull, MA 02045
(781) 925-9739
hullyc.org

Jeffries Yacht Club
565 Sumner St.
East Boston, MA 02128
(617) 500-7865

Nantasket Beach Salt Water Club
3 Fitzpatrick Way
Hull, MA 02045
(781) 925-9801
nbswc.org

Old Colony Yacht Club
235 Victory Rd.
Dorchester, MA 02122
(617) 436-0513
oldcolonyyc.org

Orient Heights Yacht Club
61 Bayswater St.
Boston, MA 02128
(617) 567-9439
ohyc1901.com

Pleasant Park Yacht Club
562 Pleasant St.
Winthrop, MA 02152
(617) 846-7124
ppyc1910.org

Quincy Yacht Club
1310 Sea St.
Quincy, MA 02169
(617) 471-6136
quincyyachtclub.net

Savin Hill Yacht Club
400 Morrissey Blvd.
Dorchester, MA 02125
(617) 825-1108
savinhillyc.org

South Boston Yacht Club
1849 Columbia Rd.
South Boston, MA 02127
(617) 268-6132

South Shore Yacht Club
800 Bridge St.
North Weymouth, MA 02191
(781) 335-9440
ssycma.weebly.com

Squantum Yacht Club
646 Quincy Shore Dr.

Quincy, MA 02170
(617) 770-4811
squantumyc.org

Town River Yacht Club
60 Mound St.
Quincy, MA 02169
(617) 471-2716
townriveryachtclub.com

Winthrop Yacht Club
649 Shirley Sl.
Winthrop, MA 02152
(617) 846-6209
win-yc.org

Wollaston Yacht Club
692 Quincy Shore Dr.
Quincy, MA 02170
(617) 477-8448
wollastonyc.com

NONPROFITS AND MUSEUMS

Boston Harbor Now
15 State St., Suite 1100
Boston, MA 02109
(617) 223-8667
bostonharbornow.org

Friends of the Boston Harbor Islands
30 Shipyard Dr., #302
Hingham, MA 02043
(781) 740-4290
fbhi.org

Hull Lifesaving Museum
1117 Nantasket Ave.

Hull, MA 02045
(781) 925-5433
hulllifesavingmuseum.org

Mass Audubon
208 South Great Rd.
Lincoln, MA 01773
(781) 259-9500
massaudubon.org

New England Aquarium
1 Central Wharf
Boston, MA 02110
(617) 973-5200
neaq.org

Save the Harbor/Save the Bay
Boston Fish Pier
212 Northern Ave., Suite 304 West
Boston, MA 02210
(617) 451-2860
savetheharbor.org

Thompson Island Outward Bound
Education Center
P.O. Box 127
Boston, MA 02127
(617) 328-3900
thompsonisland.org

The Trustees of Reservations
200 High St.
Boston, MA 02110
(617) 542-7696
thetrustees.org

MANAGEMENT AGENCIES AND OTHER GOVERNMENTAL RESOURCES

Boston City Archaeology Program
City Archaeologist
201 Rivermoor St.
West Roxbury, MA 02132
(617) 635-3850
boston.gov/departments/archaeology

Boston Harbor Islands National & State Park
15 State St., Suite 1100
Boston, MA 02109
(617) 223-8666
nps.gov/boha

Boston Harbor Islands Welcome Center
191 W Atlantic Ave.
Boston, MA 02110
(617) 223-8666

Town of Hingham Harbormaster
28 Shipyard Dr.
Hingham, MA 02043
(781) 741-1450
hpd.org/198/Harbormaster

Town of Hull Harbormaster
Hull Town Hall
253 Atlantic Ave.
Hull, MA 02045
(781) 925-0316
town.hull.ma.us/harbormaster

Massachusetts Board of Underwater
Archaeological Resources
251 Causeway St., Suite 800
Boston, MA 02114
(617) 626-1200
mass.gov/czm/buar

Massachusetts Department of Conservation and Recreation
251 Causeway St., 9th Fl.
Boston, MA 02114
(617) 626-1250
mass.gov/dcr

Massachusetts Environmental Police
Coastal Bureau
30 Shipyard Dr., Building 45
Hingham, MA 02043
(781) 740-1163
mass.gov/orgs/massachusetts-envi
ronmental-police-coastal-bureau

Massachusetts Port Authority
Maritime Department
700 Summer St.
South Boston, MA 02127
(800) 294-2791
massport.com

Massachusetts Water Resources
Authority
Charlestown Navy Yard
100 First Ave.
Boston, MA 02129
(617) 242-6000
mwra.com

NOAA Fisheries
55 Great Republic Dr.
Gloucester, MA 01930
(978) 281-9300
nmfs.noaa.gov

City of Quincy Harbormaster
Houghs Neck Maritime Center
137 Bayview Rd.
Quincy, MA 02169
(617) 745-5896
quincyma.gov/govt/depts/
harbormaster

United States Coast Guard
Sector Boston
427 Commercial St.
Boston, MA 02109
(617) 223-3123 (primary)
(617) 223-5757 (emergency only)
uscg.mil

Town of Weymouth Harbormaster
275 River St.
North Weymouth, MA 02191
(781) 682-6109
weymouth.ma.us/harbormaster

Town of Winthrop Harbormaster
The Town Landing
707 Shirley St.
Winthrop, MA 02152
(617) 207-9092

Acknowledgments

This book was a pleasure to write, not just because of the many glorious days spent on the Boston Harbor Islands, but because of the people I met along the way. I can only hope that their passion for the islands comes across on these pages.

My particular thanks go to Union Park Press for originally publishing this book in 2008 and to Nicole Vecchiotti for her tireless work in producing the first two editions. Thanks also to Sarah Parke, who edited this new third edition, and to all of the staff at Globe Pequot Press for their interest in updating this Boston Harbor Islands guidebook.

Thank you to all who have shared their limitless knowledge, photographs, and, most important, love of the Boston Harbor Islands and to the librarians and archivists who assisted me in researching their history.

Enjoy your island adventures!

About the Author

Christopher Klein is the author of four books, including *When the Irish Invaded Canada* and *Strong Boy: The Life and Times of John L. Sullivan*. A frequent contributor to History.com, the website of the History Channel, Christopher has also written for *The Boston Globe*, *The New York Times*, *National Geographic Traveler*, *Harvard Magazine*, Smithsonian.com, and AmericanHeritage.com. He lives in Andover, Massachusetts, and can be found online at christopherklein.com.

ALSO BY CHRISTOPHER KLEIN

When the Irish Invaded Canada: The Incredible True Story of the Civil War Veterans Who Fought for Ireland's Freedom
Strong Boy: The Life and Times of John L. Sullivan, America's First Sports Hero
The Die-Hard Sports Fan's Guide to Boston: A Spectator's Handbook